Keep The Wheel Turning

Keep The Wheel Turning

Journals & Letters on a Bowing Pilgrimage

by

Heng Sure Ph.D.
and
Heng Ch'au Ph.D.

Volume Six

Buddhist Text Translation Society
Dharma Realm Buddhist University
Dharma Realm Buddhist Association
Burlingame, California U.S.A.

Keep The Wheel Turning
Journals & Letters on a Bowing Pilgrimage. Volume Six.

Published and translated by:

Buddhist Text Translation Society
1777 Murchison Drive, Burlingame, CA 94010-4504

First edition 2007

16 15 14 13 12 11 10 09 08 07   12 11 10 9 8 7 6 5 4 3 2

ISBN 978-0-88139-911-0

Printed in Malaysia.

Note: Contents selected from previously published title "Open Your Eyes Take a Look at the World."

Addresses of the Dharma Realm Buddhist Association branches are listed at the back of this book.

Library of Congress Cataloging-in-Publication Data

Heng Sure, 1949-
  Keep the wheel turning / by Heng Sure and Heng Ch'au.
    p. cm. -- (Journals & letters on a bowing pilgrimage ; v. 6)
  ISBN 978-0-88139-911-0 (hard cover : alk. paper)
  1. Spiritual life--Buddhism. 2. Heng Sure, 1949- 3. Heng Ch'au. 4.
Buddhist pilgrims and pilgrimages--California. I. Heng Ch'au. II.
Title. III. Series.

  BQ5625.H465 2007
  294.3'43509794--dc22

2007002698

Contents

Preface

Three steps, one bow – three steps along the side of the highway, then a bow to the ground, so that knees, elbows, hands, and forehead touch the earth, then rise, join the palms together, and take three more steps, then begin another bow. Hour after hour, day after day, for two and a half years, this was how they made their pilgrimage. In China, devout Buddhists sometimes undertake the arduous and prayerful practice of three steps, one bow, for the last few hundred yards of a journey to a sacred site. But this was California, and these two pilgrim-monks were young Americans. Dressed in their robes and sashes, carrying no money, armed with nothing but discipline and reverence, they walked and bowed 800 miles along the narrow shoulder of the Pacific Coast Highway. Progressing a mile a day, they bowed from downtown Los Angeles north along the coast, through Santa Barbara and along the Big Sur, through San Francisco and across the Golden Gate, then 100 miles farther north to the City of Ten Thousand Buddhas, a newly founded religious and educational center in Mendocino County. As they bowed, their prayer was that the world would be free of disaster, calamity, and war.

The silent monk in the lead was Heng Sure. Originally from Toledo, Ohio, he had found his way in 1974 to Gold Mountain Buddhist Monastery in San Francisco. There on a side street of the Mission District, an eminent Chinese monk, the Venerable Master

Hsuan Hua, was living in obscurity as he carried out his pioneering work of transplanting the Buddhist monastic tradition to the West. Moved by Master Hua's virtue and wisdom, Heng Sure joined other young Americans in taking a monastic name and the full ordination of a Buddhist monk.

During his subsequent studies, Heng Sure read of a bowing pilgrimage made in the 1880's by the Venerable Hsu Yun ("Empty Cloud"), who was the most distinguished Chinese monastic of his generation. Master Yun had bowed every third step across the breadth of China; it had taken him five years. Heng Sure knew that Master Yun had been patriarch of the Wei Yang Lineage of the Chan School, and he knew that his own abbot and teacher, Master Hua, was the current patriarch, having received the lineage transmission from Master Yun in 1949. Inspired by this close connection, Heng Sure asked Master Hua if he could undertake his own pilgrimage of three steps, one bow. Master Hua approved, but said, "Wait."

Heng Sure had to wait a year. What he needed, Master Hua said, was the right companion and protector. It was to be Heng Chau. Originally from Appleton, Wisconsin, Heng Chau had come to Berkeley to study martial arts, and he had become an adept in several traditions. When his tai-chi teacher finally told him, "Chan is higher than any martial art," Heng Chau crossed the Bay to study at Gold Mountain Monastery. He soon heard about Heng Sure's vow, and he asked if he could bow with him. Within a week Heng Chau took novice precepts and made a formal vow to bow beside Heng Sure, as well as handle the logistics of cooking, cleaning, setting up camp, and talking with strangers.

Thus the pilgrimage began. Master Hua saw them off as they left Gold Wheel Monastery in Los Angeles on 7 May 1977. To Heng Chau, the martial artist, he said, "You can't use your martial arts on the pilgrimage. Heng Sure's vow is to seek an end to calamities, disasters and war; so how can you yourselves be involved in violence? If either of you fights – or even indulges in anger – you will no longer be my disciples." For protection from the dangers of the road, Master Hua instructed them to practice instead the four unconditional attitudes of the Bodhisattva: kindness, compassion, joy, and equanimity. It was by no means the last time that the two bowing monks would need their teacher's advice.

On the road, the two pilgrims followed their monastic discipline strictly – eating one vegetarian meal a day; never going indoors, sleeping sitting up in the old 1956 Plymouth station wagon that served as their shelter. In the evenings after a day of bowing they studied the Avatamsaka Sutra (Flower Adornment Sutra) by the light of an oil lamp. They translated passages into English and attempted to put into practice the principles of the text in their day-to-day experiences on the road, as their teacher had encouraged them to do. The monks guarded their concentration by avoiding newspapers, by leaving the car radio silent, and by keeping to a strict meditation schedule. Heng Sure held a vow of silence for the entire journey, and it became Heng Chau's job to talk with the many people who stopped along the highway with questions. Occasionally the visitors were hostile, and some threatened violence, but the greater number were curious, and often the curious became the monks' protectors, bringing them food and supplies until the monks had bowed their way out of range.

Everything important that happened on the highway – the mistakes and the growth, the trials and remarkable encounters, the dangers and the insights, the hard work with the body and in the mind – the pilgrims reported in letters to Master Hua. He would answer in person by visiting them from time to time, giving them indispensable spiritual guidance, admonishment, humor, and timely instructions – both lofty and mundane. These letters are the contents of this volume. They were not written with the thought that they would be published. Rather, they were a medium in which the two monks attempted to speak to their teacher as openly and sincerely as possible about their experience on the road. As such, the letters preserve an unadorned account of an authentic spiritual journey.

The Venerable Master Hsuan Hua

A Brief Portrait

"I have had many names," he once said, "and all of them are false." In his youth in Manchuria, he was known as "the Filial Son Bai"; as a young monk he was An Tzu ("Peace and Kindness"); later, in Hong Kong, he was Tu Lun ("Wheel of Rescue"); finally, in America, he was Hsuan Hua, which might be translated as "one who proclaims the principles of transformation." To his thousands of disciples across the world, he was always also "Shr Fu" – "Teacher."

Born in 1918 into a peasant family in a small village on the Manchurian plain, Master Hua was the youngest of ten children. He attended school for only two years, during which he studied the Chinese Classics and committed much of them to memory. As a young teenager, he opened a free school for both children and adults. He also began then one of his lifelong spiritual practices: reverential bowing. Outdoors, in all weathers, he would make over 800 prostrations daily, as a profound gesture of his respect for all that is good and sacred in the universe.

He was nineteen when his mother died, and for three years he honored her memory by sitting in meditation in a hut beside her grave. It was during this time that he made a resolve to go to America to teach the principles of wisdom. As a first step, at the end of the period of mourning, he entered San Yuan Monastery, took as his teacher Master Chang Chih, and subsequently received the full ordination of a Buddhist monk at Pu To Mountain. For ten years he devoted himself to study of the Buddhist scriptural tradition and to mastery of both the Esoteric and the Chan Schools of Chinese Buddhism. He had also read and contemplated the scriptures of Christianity, Taoism, and Islam. Thus, by the age of thirty, he had already established through his own experience the four major imperatives of his later ministry in America: the primacy of the monastic tradition; the essential role of moral education; the need for Buddhists to ground themselves in traditional spiritual practice and authentic scripture; and, just as essential, the importance and the power of ecumenical respect and understanding.

In 1948, Master Hua traveled south to meet the Venerable Hsu Yun, who was then already 108 years old and China's most distin-guished spiritual teacher. From him Master Hua received the patriarchal transmission in the Wei Yang Lineage of the Chan School. Master Hua subsequently left China for Hong Kong. He spent a dozen years there, first in seclusion, then later as a teacher at three monasteries which he founded.

Finally, in 1962, he went to the United States, at the invitation of several of his Hong Kong disciples who had settled in San Francisco. By 1968, Master Hua had established the Buddhist Lecture Hall in a loft in San Francisco's Chinatown, and there he began giving nightly lectures, in Chinese, to an audience of young Americans. His texts were the major scriptures of the Mahayana. In 1969, he astonished the monastic community of Taiwan by sending there, for final ordination, two American women and three American men, all five of them fully trained as novices, fluent in Chinese and conversant with Buddhist scripture. During subsequent years, the Master trained and oversaw the ordination of hundreds of monks and nuns who came to California from every part of the world to study with him. These monastic disciples now teach in the 28 temples, monasteries and convents that the Master founded in the United States, Canada, and several Asian countries.

Although he understood English well and spoke it when it was necessary, Master Hua almost always lectured in Chinese. His aim was to encourage Westerners to learn Chinese, so that they could become translators, not merely of his lectures, but of the major scriptural texts of the Buddhist Mahayana. His intent was realized. So far, the Buddhist Text Translation Society, which he founded, has issued over 130 volumes of translation of the major Sutras, together with a similar number of commentaries, instructions, and stories from the Master's teaching.

As an educator, Master Hua was tireless. From 1968 to the mid 1980's he gave as many as a dozen lectures a week, and he traveled extensively on speaking tours. At the City of Ten Thousand Buddhas in Talmage, California, he established formal training programs for monastics and for laity; elementary and secondary schools for boys and for girls; and Dharma Realm Buddhist University, together with the University's branch, the Institute for World Religions, in Berkeley.

Throughout his life the Master taught that the basis of spiritual practice is moral practice. Of his monastic disciples he required strict purity, and he encouraged his lay disciples to adhere to the five precepts of the Buddhist laity. Especially in his later years, Confucian texts were often the subject of his lectures, and he held to the Confucian teaching that the first business of education is moral education. He identified six rules of conduct as the basis of communal life at the City of Ten Thousand Buddhas; the six rules prohibit contention, covetousness, self-seeking, selfishness, profiting at the expense of the community, and false speech. He asked that the children in the schools he had founded recite these prohibitions every morning before class. In general, although he admired the independent-mindedness of Westerners, he believed that they lacked ethical balance and needed that stabilizing sense of public morality which is characteristic of the East.

The Venerable Master insisted on ecumenical respect, and he delighted in inter-faith dialogue. He stressed commonalities in religious traditions – above all their emphasis on proper conduct, on compassion, and on wisdom. He was also a pioneer in building bridges between different Buddhist national traditions. He often brought monks from Theravada countries to California to share the duties of transmitting the precepts of ordination. He invited Catholic priests to celebrate the mass in the Buddha-Hall at the City of Ten Thousand Buddhas, and he developed a late-in-life friendship with Paul Cardinal Yu-Bin, the exiled leader of the Catholic Church in China and Taiwan. He once told the Cardinal: "You can be a Buddhist among the Catholics, and I'll be a Catholic among Buddhists." To the Master, the essential teachings of all religions could be summed up in a single word: wisdom.

* * *

Keep the Wheel Turning

* * * * * * * * *

U.S.A.

Heng Sure • July 27, 1978
Day 1 : San Francisco, U.S.A.

Gold Mountain is a hundred-foot pole – so easy to fall back into its silent, empty space and leak here and slide back. It's comfortable and safe.

The first night back I slipped right away and made a bee-line for my stuff, dived right in… turned by the juicer, late for bowing, missed reciting vows and *tai chi*, turned by the lunch energy, ate too fast, lost all vision; I turn the wheel only while bowing and sitting.

Only after worrying and hassling the baggage and people did I realize I don't have to do any of this garbage. It is just the old game and you are not here any more. Your new job is to keep bowing and keep working. You can do it.

Gold Mountain was familiar, but only like a photo album. Just part of the dream. Who was it here in these narrow halls turning the millstone, happy and slowly recovering, like a convalescent patient rescued magically from a terminal ward? A passive healing, waiting for the karmic film to unreel.

On *san bu yi bai*[1], learning now to turn it, the first true, real acts of my life, coming from stillness and motion, the single source.

[1.] Three Steps, One Bow

The delegation at the San Francisco Airport

...bout to embark on a mission to Asia. July 1978.

The delegation with the Welcoming Committee

t Hoeh Beng Temple, Kuala Lumpur. July 1978.

After fifteen hours of delay, the delegation stayed pas

midnight to introduce themselves to the Welcoming Committee

Heng Chau • July 27, 1978
That's our last meal

On the plane...

The long flight and travel helps cut attachments to time and place, self and others. Travelling with the Abbot is doing the unheard of: living the Avatamsaka Sutra.

Honolulu...

We do *tai chi* in the abandoned lobby of the airport waiting for the flight to Guam.

The Abbot has been juggling the "one-meal-a-day" eating schedule to the point that I can't find the principle or the right clock to follow. It is Saturday, 9:00 a.m., Guam; 7:00 a.m., Manila; and Friday, 8:00 p.m. in San Francisco. Do we follow our stomachs, or the clock, or the airplane meal service? "We're eating our attachments," notes Heng Sure.

"That's our last meal," says the Abbot. "Tell them not to serve us anymore, Kuo T'ing." Then two hours later when they bring a meal around the Abbot says, "Eat up everyone. If we don't eat we will be hungry when we get there. Besides, the portions are really small." So what is the Abbot following? There is a teaching in all of this that I'm missing. Or, maybe that's the teaching. The steward looks at me impatiently, as if to say, "But you just told me no more meals!" I shrug my shoulders and think, "Nothing is fixed." We are all eating our attachments.

Heng Sure is always attentive to ceremonies and maintaining rites and rituals. I am just beginning to appreciate this.

Ceremonies can't be done sloppily nor ignored, right down to and including the reverent mind that does them. Cultivation is doing what you don't like because what you dislike is just what's tying you down. Bowing, being on time, following rules and rituals to the "T" – I don't like any of these. They require self-discipline and putting "me" in the back seat. Unconsciously I am always looking for loopholes and ways to get around the "way it's supposed to be done." Heng Sure's forte is right here and I'm learning a lot from him. Even though I complain, I always feel happier and more genuine after taking this bitter medicine.

Heng Sure • July 30, 1978
Day 2 : Manila / Kuala Lumpur

Manila Airport...

Imprisoned in the Manila Airport transit lounge for over nine hours. First day of no bowing in fifteen months, but my heart happy and energized, not sleepy or discouraged.

"Shih Fu, which has the real value ultimately, sitting still like the old fool as Kuo K'ung is doing, or running and doing things?"

"They all have value and they all have no value. Can you do it? That's what counts. It's not which way you go, any one method can end birth and death. Don't be so selfish."

Heng Chau • July 30, 1978
Are you sure there will be an airplane?

"Transit Building Blues"

My eyes wander and watch women. This is how I lose my light – literally "outflow." I can see what I am doing, but habit and my ignorance is deep. "Outflows come from ignorance. If ignorance is ended, there are no outflows, and the cycle of birth and death is ended." Strange that I should open a sutra and find this passage.

In flight the Abbot kept asking me all sorts of questions about arrival/departure times, etc. At one point he asked me, "Are you sure there will be an airplane for us in Manila when we get there?" I laughed, thinking it was a jab at my false thinking and trying to make "everything O.K." It was no joke. After over nine hours of delays we asked,

"What's going on?"

"Your flight has been delayed."

"Why?" we pressed.

"Mechanical difficulty."

"What kind of mechanical difficulty?"

"There's no airplane," answered an embarrassed official in a whisper.

The Abbot smiled and simply said, "Oh?"

There were strange forces at work regarding the Manila "flight delay." It was clearly on the faces of all the officials there. Later we found out that all our messages and cablegrams sent during this hold-over mysteriously never arrived at their destinations. The Abbot commented later, "Your *ding li* (concentration power) was put under a strain today. Everyone did a lot of worrying. You tried not to, but it got to you all the same. You entered the 'sleeping samadhi' because of a lot of worrying. But it's o.k. Basically it's all right for me to be lazy, but my disciples can't be. That won't do. They've got to be vigorous."

And, although I told no one about my false thinking concerning women at the airport, the Abbot came out with, "Don't do so much false thinking." (to Heng Sure) "Leave that to him." (pointing to me) "He's the false thinker. Isn't that right?" I got a little nervous wondering if the Master really knew what I was doing in my head.

"Haven't you been doing a lot of false thinking?" he pressed.

"Well I, uh..."

"It's because you can't put down women yet. He still has false thoughts about women. He hasn't washed that clean yet. His habit energy is still heavy."

The Abbot knew.

> "The Buddha in the playful Samadhi teaches living beings
> as if nothing were going on."
>
> Earth Store Sutra

* * * * * * * * *

Malaysia

July 30, 1978
Hoeh Beng Temple – Kuala Lumpur

The Abbot's arrival address to about six hundred people at Hoeh Beng Temple:

"The Buddhism we practice is Universal Buddhism, not a Buddhism that is limited by nationality, race, creed, or social status. It is, rather, a faith that extends to the ends of the Dharmarealm and Empty Space. This is the Space Age now, a new age. We cannot shut ourselves in anymore. We have to expand and open up widely to embrace worlds as numerous as dust motes in the universe."

* * *

An excerpt of the Abbot's speech during the packed evening Earth Store Dharma Assembly at the Chinese Assembly Hall, Selangor:

"I am a horse – a horse carrying a load of people to Malaysia. The disciples always excel the teacher, and I firmly believe that. I want to walk last – behind all Buddhist disciples. In fact, I wish to walk underneath the feet of all Buddhists. You see, I am an ant."

The Chinese Assembly Hall

Kuala Lumpur, Malaysia. 1978.

The large crowd at the Chinese Assembly Ha

...attending the Earth Store Dharma Assembly

People listened with rapt attention to the

Venerable Master and his disciples speak Dharma

July 31, 1978
Day 3 : Brickfields / Petaling Jaya

At Brickfields:

Question: "What is the difference between the Mahayana and Theravada traditions?"

The Abbot: "There is basically no difference in the ideals that the Buddha taught, so why should we haggle over Mahayana and Theravada, each disclaiming the other? Mahayanists belittle the Theravadans, the Theravadans do not respect the Mahayanists. Anyone who seeks to divide Buddhism from within is not worthy of being called a Buddhist disciple. Not to talk about the greater or lesser vehicle, there isn't even one vehicle in this case! These people bank on the name Buddhism to wreak havoc and sow seeds of discontentment and warfare. I say to my disciples, 'If you ever make discriminations between the Northern and Southern schools like this, you aren't my disciples at all!'"

During a refuge ceremony at Dharma Master Po Yuen's temple (*Hu Pin Ching Shieh*), the Master gave the following talk:

"By taking refuge with me, you have taken refuge with the Triple Jewel. You shouldn't start making discriminations between this Dharma Master and that. After a person has taken refuge with me, if he still disrespects or slanders other Sanghans, then he is not a true disciple of mine. A true disciple of mine has taken refuge with the Permanently Dwelling Sangha of the Ten Directions. Don't make discriminations in your giving. Don't say, 'This Dharma Master is high and lofty, I'll make more offerings to him,' or 'This Dharma Master is not as virtuous, I won't plant blessings with him.' Don't make this kind of distinction. Most importantly do not slander the Triple Jewel. You should all draw near to, respect, and honor the Good Knowing Advisors all over Malaysia. Today is the beginning of a new life for you. Turn over a new leaf. Be a new person. Put aside your old habits – all that greed, anger, and stupidity. After taking refuge, you should be strong, upright Buddhist disciples, not just Buddhists in name only. Make yourselves models for the world to see. If you want to remain ordinary people, don't take refuge with me.

"I will tell you of a stupid vow I made a long time ago. When I was still a Shramanera, people from the nearby villages in China wished to take refuge with me. Considering my own lack of virtue, I made a vow that all my disciples must become Buddhas before I do. So, I'm waiting for all of you to quickly cultivate and realize Buddhahood. You wouldn't want to keep your teacher waiting, would you?"

In the afternoon, at the Karma Kaygu Dharma Center:
(the Abbot lectures on the incredible functions of the Shurangama Mantra and the Great Compassion Mantra)

"Many scholars claim that the Shurangama Sutra is not authentic – that it did not come from the Buddha's mouth. Actually, it is the single most important sutra. As long as it stays in the world, the Proper Dharma will remain. As soon as the Shurangama Sutra and Mantra disappear from this world system, the heavenly demons and those of outside-way sects will overrun it at will. Then the Proper Dharma will vanish and darkness will cover the entire world.

"Many scholars now arguing the Shurangama Sutra's alleged lack of authenticity are the children of demons disguised as academicians in order to confuse people and divert their faith in the Orthodox Canon. I can vouch for the authenticity of the Shurangama Sutra, I vow to fall into the hells forever if this sutra did not truly come from the Buddha's mouth. Unless you think I am stupid, you should know by my vow that I am sincere in this.

"The Shurangama Mantra has functions too wonderful and numerous to relate here, but in general, there are five functions: the dharma of accomplishment, the dharma of increasing benefit, the dharma of dispelling disasters, the dharma of hooking and summoning, and the dharma of subduing.

"The Shurangama Mantra is the most powerful and highest of the dharmas transmitted by the Buddha. It alone can subdue even the most lethal of demons and external paths."

The Abbot answers a question from the audience:

Q: "What is your opinion of test-tube babies?"

A: "The beginning of the extinction of the human race!"

(The whole house is in stitches; the next day it is all over the papers.)

Heng Sure • July 31, 1978
Full of a special, holy energy

Arrival.

Strong feeling of being at home in Kuala Lumpur – the market, the late-night food stands, the warmth of the Chinese laymen, the power of the two high monks, the languages, the pressure of the Muslim country, wide-open and free, and we with a mission.

Morning recitation in the public Buddha Hall of Hoeh Beng Monastery. There's a feeling in the air of spirits and Dharma-protectors startled from long slumber by the sounds of the bell and fish. With the ceremony the atmosphere has been revitalized immeasurably. The Abbot stresses regular performance of morning and evening devotions in all of his Way-places. No wonder many Buddhists say that Gold Mountain Monastery and Tathagata Monastery, Gold Wheel Temple and the Institute are full of a special, holy energy.

Heng Chau • July 31, 1978
Hot, crowded and tight

The heat and the sun are hard to take in Kuala Lumpur: crowded with living beings sharing tight spaces. The Hoeh Beng Temple accommodates ants, roaches, "wall tigers" (lizards that roam the walls and ceilings), people, rats, cats, and many more that one can feel but not see. The sun rises and sets, but the heat doesn't move.

Press interviews, lots of visiting sangha, large crowds and speeches, yet somehow we are not feeling uptight. Why? The Abbot generates an easy, relaxed manner, and the heat is subdued. But also, it's coming to see the emptiness of worldly dharmas and oneself. What counts can't be seen; what matters can't be told. Cultivating the self-nature and the Way-virtue that comes from deep and true practice is where it's at.

Opening Night: over 1,500 people.

Malaysian Minister of Health gives welcoming address – unprecedented in a Muslim country where most religions and public activities are banned. "Small miracle," say local politicos. The Abbot begins:

"I bow to all you worthy people… leave if you're tired, but if you stay you have to listen, whether you like what I say or not… To all of you I ask a simple question: 'How are you?' You're all fine, but I'm not fine. Why? Because I am one who can't speak. But I'll force it and do what I can't do. My mouth is clumsy, and my mind is not bright…"

The Abbot drops "A-bombs" on people's minds. A few nervous folks squirm in their seats as the Abbot says, "Buddhism includes all religions," implying Islam, too.

On the way back to the temple the Abbot listens to the nervous responses and calmly says,

"I'm just telling it like it is. Good medicine is bitter to the taste. I just want to help people expand the measure of their minds."

"There will be even more people tomorrow night," the laymen excitedly say. "This is the first time we've heard the Dharma like this! Tomorrow night will be standing-room only. Malaysia has never had a real Dharma assembly – this is historic!"

On Filiality.

Why would young Americans "leave home"? Why would they give up the most affluent lifestyle in the world to become monks and nuns who eat one simple meal a day and never lie down? To do something old-fashioned and basic to being a person: to repay the kindness of their parents.

The most advanced discoveries of the West are beginning to prove empirically what the Ancients knew centuries before us: we are all one substance and one nature: the Universe is non-dual.

Einstein's Law of the Conservation of Matter and Energy states that nothing is produced or destroyed. The whole of the Universe is one substance that is constantly in flux – simply changing form. A star, an animal, a person, and a water molecule mutually share the same matter and interfuse. The Heart Sutra states the same principle:

> Form does not differ from emptiness;
> Emptiness does not differ from form.
> The very form is emptiness;
> The very emptiness is form...
>
> All dharmas are empty of appearances,
> Neither produced nor destroyed;
> Neither defiled nor pure;
> Neither increasing nor decreasing.

Einstein made his discoveries in the last forty years. The Heart Sutra is over three thousand years old.

The Ancients used this understanding of the oneness of all things to bring forth minds of great compassion. They saw all things as their body – they took all beings as their parents. Modern science has used this understanding to bring forth great destruction and a mind that seeks self-benefit. The world is a mess of wars, disasters, and suffering because we don't recognize our parents. We don't know our brothers and sisters.

This is the attraction that the Buddhadharma holds for young Westerners. How can we learn to live with the atomic bomb and freak out over a shaved head?

"In America I am doing your work," said the Venerable Abbot.

"Here I am working on your behalf," replied Sri Dhammananda.

"In fact, we all work for the Buddha," replied the Abbot, "and we must actually go and do our best. Narrow sectarian views can no longer stand. Basically there are no sects or vehicles."

Food and Desire:

External changes	Internal changes
people!	no mental clarity
talking	sloppy sitting
the food	no sutra
the schedule	no circulation
the weather	desire thoughts
Gold Mountain friends	no effort connects

Dharma Master Po Yuen welcomes the

Venerable Master to Hu Pin Ching Shieh

A refuge ceremony follows after lunch, durin

which about three-hundred people took refuge

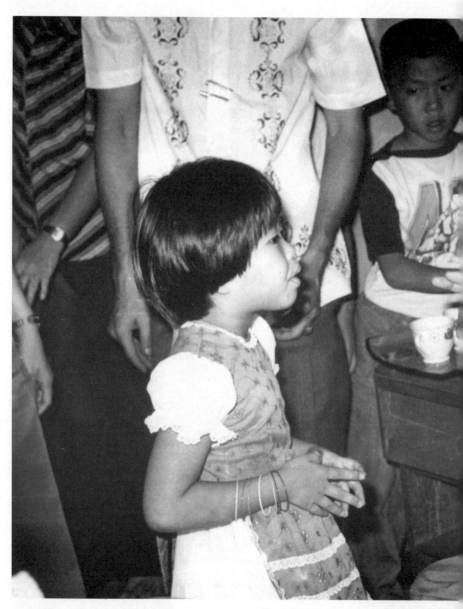

The Venerable Master tirelessly imparts

Dharma treasures to people of all ages

A group portrait of the delegation and disciples

at Hu Pin Ching Shieh, Petaling Jaya, 1978.

A larger group photo of the delegation at

Hu Pin Ching Shieh, Petaling Jaya, 1978

Heng Sure • August 1, 1978
Day 4 : Meditate before speaking the Dharma

Heng Ch'au to Heng Sure: "You have turned into a stick of wood. People at lunch are already beginning to look right past you. Put down the impulse to get involved in the conversation."

If Heng Ch'au can put down his interest in hearing what is said (that does not pertain to him or me), I should be able to concentrate on my eating, and subduing desire. I will dead-bird it totally and just not talk.

Dharma Master Huei Seng: "It's really best to meditate before speaking the Dharma. You can have a stack of materials prepared and when it's time to talk, if you haven't meditated, it all disappears. You can have no material, but after sitting the material arrives by itself."

Heng Ch'au: "Where do the women come from?"

Dharma Master Huei Seng: "They see your Way-practices and they make a bee-line for it."

Kuo K'ung: "I really dislike having my picture taken."

Abbot: "That's also one of my preferences – I don't like my image to run away into that little mirror-box. Now I will sit still for pictures because I practice doing what I don't like to do. But before this, Kuo Chen knows, whenever people took my photo, the picture wouldn't come out. Funny, but it happened time and again. The film was just blank."

August 2, 1978
Day 5 : The cheapest, most expensive item on earth

The Abbot on greed:

"So far many people have come to see me. All want something: if it is not greed for personal benefit, it is greed for fame, or greed for some secret dharma. Rarely does a person come just for the sake of truth. Nobody wants to give something to Buddhism. They all want Buddhism to give something to them.

"However, the more you want, the less you are able to get. It is a simple law of logic: your greed obstructs true receptivity. You cannot be a true Dharma Vessel unless you are empty. Dharma is the 'cheapest' thing on earth, for there is no worldly value that can be attached to it; by the same token, it is also the most expensive item, for no amount of money can buy what the heart transmits. If you are willing to look within, you'll discover limitless treasures within your own self-nature."

To the hundreds of people who come to the Abbot for cures of their illnesses, the Abbot says,

"I am not a doctor. I don't usually meddle in people's affairs, but only on occasion do I help those who are suffering deeply. The best help you can get is your attendance at the Dharma lectures. The Buddhas and Bodhisattvas help those who help themselves."

Heng Sure • August 2, 1978
There's still a lot that turns you

Lunch at the Kaygupa Center… couldn't withstand the pressure… doing everything right – all controls on and working – and I still automatically acted, took action and upset everything.

Heng Sure: "Shih Fu, we're not seeking fame in our work, we just want to realize our vow."

Abbot: "Well, Kuo Chen, you'd better die a little sooner then. If you don't have a name in your heart, then who is there to seek? Who am I? I don't have a name – who seeks?"

After lunch, high desire pushed me further and further under wraps. Smaller and smaller consciousness – couldn't breathe or smile or relax.

Abbot: "How did you sleep? Dizzy?"

Heng Ch'au: "Still weak."

Abbot: "Don't have a self. Forget yourself. With no self, who can get dizzy? Any experiences while bowing?"

Heng Ch'au: "I fell asleep on stage."

Heng Sure: "I had a lot of desire thoughts for the first time in months."

Abbot: "It's because you still don't recognize states. There's still a lot that turns you; your samadhi power is insufficient."

Heng Sure: "I haven't sat now for too long. Finally last night I got in some long sitting."

Abbot: "Do your very best to keep your own schedule going. Even if all you do with us is eat lunch, that's okay. Even to the point that if you want them to fix something special for you at lunch… that could be arranged."

Ask for plain food – raw: rice and fruit, and greens and vegies, and whole grains.

Haven't entered stillness for a week. Feels just like Gold Wheel weekends. The difference is the food.

San bu yi bai eats simple food. The same diet day after day. Not very much. Controlled down to the last bite. Really quiet and concentrated. Relaxed. A list of rules is repeated every day:

Menu: Fruit, canned food – very little cooked food; no heat,
no oil, no sugar, no flavor; crackers, dried food, simple, raw;
whole grains, vegetables, tofu; nuts, cheese, seeds, cereal.

We can't eat cooked dishes. Solutions:

Not meet offerings;
Carry our own;
Eat less (not enough fuel).

Is this an attachment? Will others get jealous? Should we just bear it? We eat what others can't eat. Should we just eat less? It seems to make a big difference. Solutions:

Eat only what will help bowing;
Don't eat the dishes our desire wants;
Request rice;
Be sincere about ending food desire.

The Abbot compassionately intervened; they brought out big plates of raw vegies and sliced pineapple, carrots, cauliflower, cabbage, and fruit.

"You can write out a menu and ask for what you like," he said.

We passed the extra portion to the middle of the table.

"I'll eat whatever you can't handle," he said, and did just that.

Oily, fried rice appeared, and Dharma Master Huei Seng said,

"No, no, they can't eat that."

"No, take it away," gestured the Abbot with a wave of his hand. "When they do *san bu yi bai* they eat the weeds that grow by the roadside. Really simple stuff," he said to Dharma Master Huei Seng.

"Tell them about your thoughts, your false thoughts," said the Abbot. "Tell Dhammananda, he didn't get your Chinese; repeat it for him."

Later the Abbot asked, "What's on your mind?"

"Lot's of desire thoughts, Shih Fu, for the first time in months. Heavy and sticky."

"There's something turning you. You don't recognize a state that has come up. Your samadhi power is insufficient."

As we bowed on the stage behind the Abbot's Dharma Seat, I saw a woman appear beside me. She was waving her arms and reaching for me. She bowed to the cushion and didn't rise, then she stepped back and moved her body seductively. After fifteen minutes of this her family came and carried her off the stage.

We drove home after the lecture. The Abbot's first words were, "See what your desire thoughts called in? That woman is a heavenly demon. Your desire thoughts opened the door for her. I broke her dharma, so she couldn't get to you."

Heng Chau • August 2, 1978
Lighting up like a Christmas tree

> As a bee is greedy for good honey,
> So, too, do we in just that way,
> Wish to hear these Dharmas of sweet dew.
>
> Avatamsaka Sutra

Like hungry bees, people come to absorb the proper Dharma. Each day the doubts and calluses of lost faith drop away. A tidal wave of unprecedented enthusiasm is building. At night Heng Sure and I bow on the stage next to the Dharma seat. Behind us we can hear the hearts crack open as the Abbot turns the wonderful Dharma Wheel. The assembly hall fills up with a white-blue-golden light, and by the end, each person present is beside himself with excited happiness and covered with Dharma light.

Here in Kuala Lumpur, the bell and fish and bowing cushions are rusty and dusty, the icons and altars dull and dormant. But every place the Abbot and delegation goes lights up like a Christmas tree, as the sounds and pulse of the Buddhadharma chase out the rats and dust and gather in bright-eyed disciples.

But, internal is the real revolution. The real purpose of the mission is small – very small. It's as small as a single thought. And that single thought is the "thought for the Way; the resolve for Bodhi."

People here are moved by what they hear and see. The Abbot is a mirror within which they see their true natures – reflections in the Wish-fulfilling Pearl. You and I are not two, we are one. Malaysia and America are one, not two. The ocean separates or unites according to one's attitude – the water knows no difference.

The Abbot totally steers clear of all the praise and pomp:

> Without the slightest wavering,
> his Ch'an concentration is profound.
>
> Avatamsaka Sutra

The Venerable Abbot has no desire to be worshipped or held up as a savior. "I want my disciples to have wisdom, not superstition. Follow yourself, don't follow me."

Heng Sure • August 3, 1978
Day 6 : It is for certain, but nothing is fixed

Abbot: "How was the eating? Okay? Did you get enough? You should eat your fill. Don't undereat on purpose. To force undereating is to be off the middle. Not enough is the same as too much. You should eat a little more.

"Cultivation is not choosing food; just eat your fill. Don't cheat yourself.

"Nothing is fixed. Just that is Anuttarasamyaksambodhi."

Heng Ch'au: "Shih Fu, you say cause and effect is for certain, but nothing is fixed. How is this?"

Abbot: "It is not fixed that you don't have to cultivate. It means that you choose the right path – you go toward the good. It doesn't mean you can kill and steal. Nothing is fixed means to go to the good. Do no evil, offer up good conduct. Have no attachments.

"It means you certainly must cultivate.

"What I said was simple and brief, but there was lots of important principle within it. Telling people not to call vegetables mock-meat – this is just to tell people to go to the true and not be false."

I have been attaching to the state of good meditation and reduced desire by attaching to emptiness. This is false, feeling that it is righteous to force hunger.

I can endure a harsh self-restriction, but I can't bear to face desire straight on. I have reduced the fire to a spark and considered it a victory. What I need is to build a foundry with a blast-furnace that can control any amount of heat. Control, not avoidance.

I have been cheating myself – living as an ascetic recluse. Now that I'm back in society, my desire is as strong as ever, multiplied by hunger. I haven't dealt with the truth. I have taken a side road.

What I have done is to go for the small, for the quick. Trying to end desire by attaching to emptiness. Trying to starve in the Himalayas. The Middle Way is to get control and be strong.

What is the truth of my food dilemma? I am too thin and too weak. I look devitalized and emaciated. This is not the way to represent the Buddhadharma.

At the same time it could be a big test – is Heng Sure really sincere about ending desire – enough that he will forsake appearances and comfort for the sake of the Way?

I don't think it's a test, because undereating is not the Way. Eating once a day it's necessary to eat one's fill. My stomach has shrunk to pea-size; it gets full in a hurry. If what I put in it is tasty, rich food, then I will surely never be clear or clean. If I fill it with bland fuel and slowly expand its capacity back to a balanced middle, then will have both strength, resilience, and the clarity I need to really cultivate the long, patient, hard path.

Abbot: "No, no, eat your fill – too little is the same as too much. Eating too little is not the Buddhadharma."

Heng Sure: "I'm really too thin – like a hungry ghost."

Abbot: "Yes, you should eat more. When you run out of gas, you stop moving."

Heng Sure: "But I don't like to keep everyone waiting at the table."

Abbot: (change of expression) "You're still using effort on the surface of things. Whether people wait or not is not your concern. You can even eat on after *gung yang* (meal ending chant) is over. No problem."

Heng Sure: "I've always equated ending desire with stopping eating altogether."

Abbot: "No – just eat your fill once. Where is there desire in that?"

Heng Chau • August 3, 1978
The problem is inside, not in Kuala Lumpur

Despite warnings in dreams and hints from the Abbot, we've cultivated *san bu yi bai* into a tailspin dive (Heng Sure and I feel). Why? We lacked the samadhi power to turn the states of weather, food, new roles, and lots of attention. We have been bowing in the wilderness – eating and bowing in solitude only a few days ago.

But everything is made from the mind. It's the mind of desire and small wisdom that attaches to states and makes a mess: the problem is inside, not in Kuala Lumpur or Big Sur.

"Your merit and virtue has run away, but don't worry, it will return," quipped the Abbot.

The meaning is that I scattered my energy into food, women, talking, and gawking and spent all my savings like a drunken sailor in port.

"You no longer can afford to be like others. You are already different. It is like climbing a steep mountain at this point – you are struggling for each foothold, for every inch," instructed the Abbot.

Each day the temple here in Kuala Lumpur gets cleaner and more people appear. Floors are mopped, incense urns and glass windows are cleaned and polished. Flowers carefully arranged in the altars. Springtime of the self-nature wherever the Dharma sounds. Bodhi seeds are popping open. "When the mind is purified, the Buddhaland is purified."

"Custom breaking"

The more we travel and exchange views, the more I see that Buddhism is flourishing on the frontier, in the West. In Asia, the Buddhadharma had degenerated into a hodgepodge of superstition, empty ritualism, and narrow sects that fight and vie for offerings, disciples.

Vegetarian "meat" is soy or wheat products that are spiced up and advertised as mock chicken, pork, beef, etc. The appeal is to flavor and the "down-home aroma of Mom's chicken." Says the Master after one such meal, "This is still the killing mind and greed for flavor. We should be clear about this."

August 4, 1978
Day 7 : Buddhist Society – Port Klang, Basang

In a large open courtyard before a crowd of about eight hundred, the Abbot speaks against superstitious practices that have undermined Buddhism:

"Is Buddhism just burning large chunks of incense and being greedy for wealth, long life and children? All you end up doing is turning the Buddha's bodies black with incense smoke. Originally the Buddhas' bodies are golden-colored; I don't know in this case whether your offenses are heavier than your merit. Don't gauge the Buddha's appetite by your own greedy minds. Do you think the Buddhas are so greedy for incense that they have to gulp it down in big mouthfuls? If not, then why are you burning joss sticks left and right until the Way-places are entirely reeking with smoke?

"And as for paper money – some people are so smart that they think they can prepare a cash-reserve for themselves in the lower realms. Why don't you work towards the Western Paradise instead of the hells? You spend all this time on paper houses and airplanes to no avail. All I know is that after these are burned they become a pile of ashes, that's all. Do you think ghosts can really enjoy these items? Ghosts are a form of energy, they have no corporeal bodies like us humans. They have no need for money and physical comforts. If they cultivate, they can also become Buddhas. Do not be confused about ghosts. I often say,

> In the West there are poor ghosts;
> In the East there are no rich gods.

Why? In the West, people don't burn paper money for the deceased – does this mean the ghosts there are all poor? And in the East people don't burn money as offerings to the gods – that is why I say they are not rich in your region." (laughter and cheers)

The Venerable Master exhorts the crow

efore a large open courtyard in Klang

Heng Sure • August 4, 1978
The heavenly demon takes refuge

A woman had been poisoned by *lwo gang tou*, the "gu poison," a very serious, fatal poisoning which can be caught in many ways. It goes down inside and swells up and you die.

She feared the Abbot's face, could not look at him. She could not listen to sutras.

The heavenly demon came to take refuge with the Abbot.

"She came to follow me, she wants to take refuge. She and all the others – they wore blue clothes, some in red, some in white, some in yellow clothes. You didn't see them?" he asked with a gently mocking laugh.

If I feel there's not enough time to get back into the middle, then I should quit. Time doesn't exist!

How fast we go! How much we take for granted. False thoughts and attachments override the richness of existence. Expectations, recollections, projected onto the world obscuring the present moment which is always full of wonder.

A thermos bottle full of tea is a complex system of changes and forces. An offering of rice is the peak of a tall pyramid of human effort.

A big bowl of soupy noodles with vegetables!

Currents of heat running up and down my body, it registers as desire. In fact, it's just new unchannelled energy. Meditation and bowing directs it and controls it, for a while.

Empty, hungry, on fire – can feel my extra flesh and inner reserves burning to keep the work going – consuming and smelting my body as fuel. Really uncomfortable.

All suffering I take on behalf of living beings. All happiness I give away to all living beings. The Dharma is the refuge – a cool wind to release the fear and pain. With no self to seek, what is there to fear? Who is there to worry?

Abbot: "You should know that in these last few days you haven't applied your skill well. I expect it's because you have been confused by being close to so many women. You have been turned by states, so start over – smelt again. If you lose the battle, go back to war."

August 5, 1978
Day 8 : Brickfields / University Malaya – Kuala Lumpur

The Abbot's address at University of Malaya:

"You are all energetic, capable young people, bound to do great things in the world. You are our future leaders and models, so don't take yourselves lightly, nor the hope I entrust upon you. I wish to sign a contract with you: that you pursue true principle above all else.

"Last night we discussed confused belief (superstition) at Klang. There is 'confused belief' and 'belief in confusion.' In the former case there is still hope, for here, although people follow superstitious customs, they still have some faith, and their faith can be ameliorated into belief in something true. The latter case – the belief in confusion – is more serious, because it means belief in deviant knowledge and views – deliberate belief in improper dharmas.

"Why are people so confused? Because they haven't the faintest idea where they come from and where they'll end up. You look at yourselves daily in the mirror and the reflection you see is not the real you. If you want the truth, you have to find out who you really are. Everybody is confused by the five desires: wealth, sex, fame, food, and sleep. I bet there is not one amongst you who has not calculated about money: 'How much money am I going to make after I get this degree? How much money can I get from a job? What pretty wife or big house can I afford?'

"Stupid or dull people, as dumb as clumps of wood or stone, do not think about money. But there are other types of people who do not think about money. They have transcended greed and are called 'sages.' Why don't sages hanker after money? Because they are already rich in internal treasures. The reason why people grab onto any tiny bit of gain and are constantly on the lookout for good bargains is that they are poor. They feel as if they don't have enough. They are always hungry. Such people are extremely pitiful, for they have lost track of their inner wealth.

"Do not be like that. Didn't I make a pact with you earlier on? Do not live as if drunk and die as if in a dream. Find out who you really are. Start out by becoming a good person: be filial to your parents, reasonable with your husband or wife, trustworthy to your colleagues. Be an honest person in society; don't live off the fat of others. Cultivating Buddhism is just this: in all you do, respectfully offer up the good, and do not do the least bit of evil. Right within everyday affairs make yourselves models. If each Buddhist can take on this responsibility, there is no fear that Buddhism will not flourish in the entire world."

At night the Abbot continues at Wisma Buddhist Association:

"It's funny how so many people came to hear this Dharma Master who's half out of his wits. I say things that nobody wants to hear, yet I can't help myself; I have to tell the truth.

"Buddhism is not delineated by countries, sects, or temples. This is the Space Age, a new era. Buddhism should go to every planet, every star. If you're still stuck to your old-fashioned ways, you will not stand up to the tests. Why should monks hoard private property, guarding their money for dear life? Why should monks seek advantages, always playing up to laypeople? If you like money so much, you shouldn't have left home in the first place. Now, what is the biggest sore spot in Buddhism? Selfishness and greed. If you work only for your own good, never thinking of sharing with all other Sanghans and Buddhists, what type of a Buddhist disciple are you? Shouldn't we reflect and ask ourselves, 'Have I really crossed over living beings? Have I cut off my afflictions? Have I helped people become Buddhas?'

"A prime minister of the Ming Dynasty once said,

> The Western Heaven is just three steps away,
> And the Eastern Sea is but one cup deep.

The Western World of Ultimate Bliss is not necessarily millions of Buddhalands away. If your mind is pure, it exists right in there. Although the Eastern Sea is vast, it is but a tiny cupful measured against the boundless, expansive sea of the self-nature. So, I'd like to alter his couplet a little and change it to,

> The Western Heaven is just half a step away,
> And the Eastern Sea is just one drop deep."

Heng Chau • August 5, 1978
I always feel I have enough of it

The Abbot doesn't play on people's superstitions and fears. He doesn't allow disciples to deify him and doesn't take their light. The Abbot teaches us how to return the light and illumine within, and stand on our own two feet. He seeks nothing, desires nothing, "Whatever it is, I always feel I have enough of it." There is no gap between what is said and what is practiced. That's half of the secret of the Abbot's success with young Americans. The other half is in his patience.

> Climbing into heaven is not hard, but teaching
>   and transforming Americans is difficult.
> Drilling through the earth is not hard, but teaching
>   and transforming Americans is difficult.
> Getting a rooster to lay eggs is not hard, but teaching
>   and transforming Americans is difficult.
>   Venerable Abbot Hua

Heng Sure helps the Venerable Master up th

airs as the Venerable Sri Dhammananda looks on

The delegation at the Brickfields Temp

...ined by the Venerable Sri Dhammananda

Heng Sure • August 6, 1978

Day 9 : Ching Yun T'ing Monastery – Malacca

Heng Ch'au: "Shih Fu, is it true that most left-home people have fallen because of money and sex?"

Abbot: "If you can separate from money and from desire then you can attain the Way."

Heng Ch'au: "I don't care so much for money, I feel."

Abbot: "Wait until you need it and then see if you can put it down."

Abbot: "All the time, everywhere – walking, dressing, eating – don't be careless or sloppy."

Abbot: "It's right before your eyes. Turn your head around and that's it. Buddhism is not obscure and marvelous.

"Bodhi is just inside afflictions. It's not outside of afflictions. It's just like ice and water, like the front and the back of your hand."

We are rich in ourselves already. We have enough.

Heng Sure: What am I doing here?

Abbot: "Even though Kuo Chen has the title of vice-chairman, it's just a name. He has no responsibility on the trip because he has resolved to cultivate.

"You two should try your very best to keep your on-the-road schedule going. The last few days you haven't been able to use effort well."

Heng Sure: I've got to get my body back and shut up and be real.

I got smacked three times today for not being straight with my words. Where has this come from?

My desire thoughts are so many, it feels like I've got a demon. It feels like a foreign and foul energy directing me from inside.

If I've caught one, it's a result of talking and breaking our *san bu yi bai* rules.

Heng Chau • August 6, 1978
You are on my radar!

The Abbot on hard work:

"I never rest. I don't know the meaning of rest. Don't assume that when I'm in my room I am resting. I'm watching every one of you on my radar, seeing what false thoughts you have... seeing you on my closed-circuit T.V. I've got all sorts of things – be careful. I need not buy them – they're all freshly made.

"And yet you still feel that running after false thoughts is permissible!"

The Abbot on Dharma greed:

"The Proper Dharma is eaten only a bit at a time. You can only put a little bit in at once. Don't be greedy for more or you'll burst your stomach."

The Ten Thousand Things are Just One...

The Abbot literally takes the Dharmarealm as his body, the invisible as his name, empty space as his school, and the four unlimited minds as his function. He puts himself below others in order to teach and transform, "I am an ant, I'm a mosquito, I'm a road. All of you walk on top of me."

All of his scolding and "atom bombs" and tireless giving come from this mind of compassion. Hard to conceive of. My mind stretches and my heart gets turned inside-out trying to embrace this. The Abbot does it effortlessly and without a single thought. Learning, learning, learning!

Heng Sure • August 7, 1978
Day 10 : A chance to disappear completely

I am uptight, because I'm seeking fame and approval from our group, from the crowd. Shih Fu is not giving me false fame with hot introductions and room to rap. He is giving us a true fame, if we can hang on to it, by putting us in a place where the only way to survive is to be absolutely true, silent, and sincere – hard work and patience.

I have a chance to disappear completely, if I dare to really do it. So far I haven't been able to. Every time a chance arrives to translate or take charge or leave my business for external affairs, I do it.

August 8, 1978
Day 11 : Hsing Liang School / Shakyan Temple

The Abbot talks about the value of time:

"Life is extremely short. Most people convince themselves that they have plenty of time, yet before they know it they have one foot in the grave, and it's too late. 'You shouldn't wait till old age to cultivate. So many lonely graves contain those who died young.' When you still have a young and healthy body, be sure to make good use of it."

The Abbot on the delegation from America:

"This group has diverse personalities, different people talented in their respective fields; they can appeal to a whole range of audiences. You can say this is an arrangement of the Bodhisattvas."

Heng Chau • August 8, 1978
Bowing is all I've done

Bowing is what I could not do when I first came to Gold Mountain. Bowing is all I've done since leaving home. Over fifteen months of bowing every day to the City of Ten Thousand Buddhas behind Heng Sure. The more we bow, the less we can talk. The less we talk, the more we understand.

Everything is impermanent.
Everything is made from the mind alone.
Everything is O.K.

Over one thousand people took refuge with the Abbot at Hoeh Beng Temple in Kuala Lumpur. So crowded – people were kneeling in the streets and courtyard outside.

August 9, 1978
Day 12 : Guan Yin is now certifying all of you

Part of the Abbot's address to his new disciples:

"Guan Yin is now at Guan Yin T"ing protecting and certifying all of you. The Buddhas and Bodhisattvas of the ten directions and the three periods of time have all come to certify you. So don't be so muddled that in coming face to face with Guan Yin you don't even recognize him. That will be too great a pity. If you take refuge as a Buddhist disciple, you should be a true one who actually practices the teaching. We should strive to be different from ordinary people. By your own example, convince other people of the truth of Buddhism."

The Venerable Master and the delegates being

shown around in Blue Cloud Pavilion Monastery

Just like old friends, the Venerable Master Hua

chats heartily with Dharma Master Chin

The Venerable Master in the Dharma seat a

Chin Yun Ting (Blue Cloud Pavilion) Monastery

佛理講座：由美國宣化老法師以

日期：一九七八年八月七日（星期一）晚

地點：群新民眾會堂（歡迎出席

The delegation at Jasir

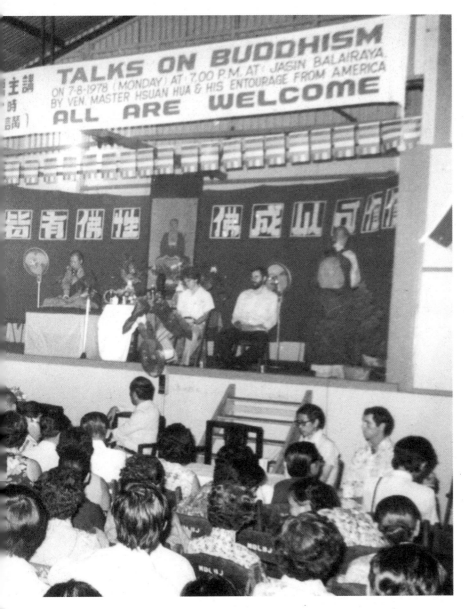

Balairaya, 7th August 1978

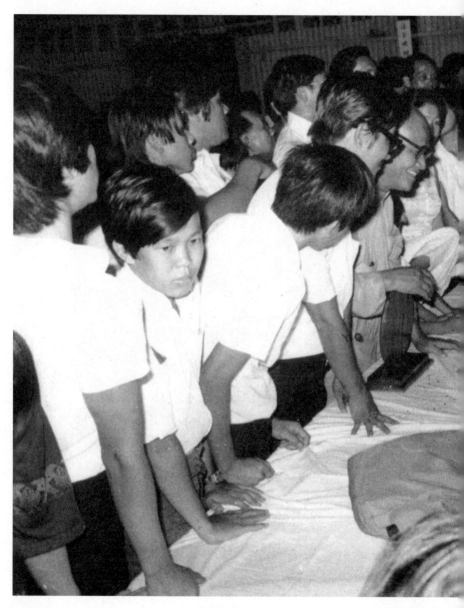

People flock to be with the Venerable Maste

...nd the delegation. Jasin, 7th August 1978.

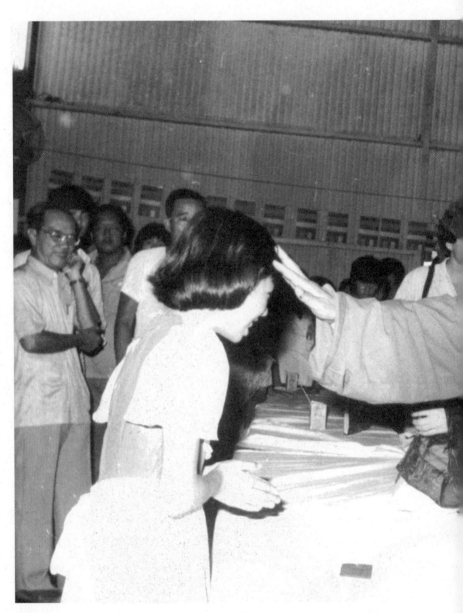

A young girl gets blessings fror

he Venerable Master Hua

Pure Karma Temple (Ching Yieh Ssu)
Muar, 10th August 1978

Heng Sure • August 9, 1978
Sleepy, heavy, no concentration

Abbot: "You two should be more independent. You needn't always accompany me. For instance, sitting in cars; you two have a little *ding li* and it's not the case that there would be any problem for you two alone."

Drawn to *yin* drinks in the heat. Trying to rebuild my wasted frame. The words fire, heat, diarrhea, fever are on everyone's lips. All the drinks have sugar – milk is everywhere – hard to avoid.

Test: drank the heavy "good" food drinks and felt hot right away. Began to sweat. Head started to nod.

Clouds covered the sharp focus adjustment in my mental screen. False thoughts like movies ran past. I felt sleepy, heavy, no concentration, no mindfulness, no light.

August 10, 1978
Day 13 : Pure Karma Temple – Muar, Johor

The Abbot on his miraculous cures of ailments:

"I'm not interested in curing people's illnesses, per se. I am not a doctor. It's just that at times when people are really sincere, a response comes from the Buddhas and Bodhisattvas, that's all."

The Abbot on how he does not permit the earth to quake in San Francisco:

"When I had finished building Hsi Le Yuan (Garden of Western Bliss) in Hong Kong, I planted some bamboos, pines, and papaya trees in the garden. After a year, the papayas started to bear very sweet fruit. That year a typhoon came and slashed all my trees and bamboos to shreds. By then I almost lost my patience, and I complained to the Jade Emperor (Lord God), saying, 'If you were responsible for this typhoon, let's get this straight. For as long as I am in Hong Kong, don't ever let any of these typhoons come again, otherwise I will not be polite with you.' And, true enough, for years whenever a typhoon would head towards the colony, it would veer off in another direction as soon as it had come to within fifteen or twenty miles of the island. In 1960, after my departure for Australia, a huge typhoon came and ripped the colony of Hong Kong apart. Later, in 1962, I went to America. The following year saw a most devastating typhoon in Hong Kong. A whole mountainside caved in at Shatin and over a hundred and fifty people were killed."

Heng Sure • August 10, 1978
The sugar and milk disease

Fight Talk for Heng Ch'au by the Abbot.

"Strike up your spirits! Don't worry! No matter how strange the goblins are, if you don't see them as strange, then they don't exist. Don't be scared.

"Even if you die, it's no problem. Every worry is put to rest then, no cares left. Whatever happens, don't see it as a problem.

"You've got to keep your happy spirits going; act as if nothing is different. Cultivators of the Way must see everything as level and equal. No matter what comes up, don't worry, don't be afraid.

"Go to war with your environment! Strike up the *t'ai chi ch'uan* vigor: Don't let circumstances change you! If you win the battle, you advance a step. If you lose the battle, you fall back a step."

As soon as I leave my own rules, I cut off my path and stumble. Purity is world-transcending. Defilement is common. At Malacca I rode a false thought through four days of suffering.

Heng Ch'au just emerged from a four-day illness. I was sick as long as he – my disease was food poisoning: sugar and milk, to be precise; his was food poisoning: spoiled fruit.

Four days of clouds, confusion, fear, desire. Stop the yin sugar input and get immediate responses.

The Abbot observes our thoughts all the time.

Every time I choose to cultivate in my mind, I get a response. For example, if there is a chance to move myself forward and speak or translate and I don't do it but dummy up and turn my wheel instead, things work out perfectly all by themselves. When I don't false think, that is.

This is the Abbot's presence at work. Each time I return the light and consult with my own inner advisor, I get the instructions I need to act correctly. False thoughts block them out!

The lessons are always these:

Accord;
Motion in stillness;
Don't act, but respond;
Stand straight;
Relax;
Give;
Be happy;
Shine the Dharma;
Benefit whoever approaches.
And most of all, first and always,
Cultivate the Way – Don't think:

Selfishness results in a scolding. My plans don't work out.

Relying on my thoughts produces an upset, a reversal. Expecting, projecting, produces "the rug being pulled out from under." Moving without cultivating, without turning the wheel produces a sharp rap, a waker-upper.

When I really step off the Path and pursue a dead-end road, I get no feedback or teaching. Then instructions come through principles delivered in lectures or Dharma talks. At this stage I have to seek out the teaching. When I use effort with a sincere heart, the instructions appear before me without being sought.

Selfishness, seeking, dreaming, falseness always fail. The Abbot reads my heart unerringly. Even a good dharma, when practiced with a false intention, becomes a loser, a bad dharma. A bad idea that comes from a good intention gets corrected, but without sting.

Back on center now, after three days of drifting in a murky yin hell of desire and discomfort. Cultivating in the Abbot's presence is electrifying – exhilarating. I can go as far as I have strength to go, but only in the right direction. Step off to one side, and the pain is fierce.

Don't think, and everything's okay!

Abbot: "In cultivation, finally you have to have no self. As long as you have a self, you've got trouble.

"Heng Ch'au is okay, huh? That's good. You don't know how serious it was. I brought him back from King Yama. It wasn't simple food poisoning. It was his old sickness uniting with external conditions. The inner poison and the outer poison joined together. It would have done him in this time."

August 11, 1978
Day 14 : Tangkak / Miao Ying Ssu – Seremban

The Abbot's speech upon arrival at Miao Ying Ssu,

"The ten people in this group can conjure up a thousand changes and transformations. They can create something from nothing and return this something to nothing again. The reason is that all these people are very different, each having his or her independent viewpoint. Now, I will use an auspicious Chinese saying to describe us: 十全十美 (completely perfect and completely beautiful). So you can see that Wonderful Response Temple is really getting a wonderful response today (applause). It is not that we are boasting. Rather, I see that the flower of Buddhism has already blossomed in Malaysia, and now we're waiting for it to bear fruit."

Heng Sure • August 11, 1978
Only their bodies have left home

> Good people never hate others.
> Sages never get angry.
> Rich people are never greedy for little advantages.
> A person of real nobility is never crude or rude.

A great person becomes that way by starting from the smallest, subtlest, most unnoticeable point. This means "not forsaking the roots and grabbing for the branches." In seeking the Buddhadharma, you need not seek far and wide. It doesn't exist tens of thousands of miles away. Real Buddhadharma is right before your very eyes in the daily transactions within mundane worldly dharmas – therein you find the Buddhadharma.

The Master's instructions.

> "Walking, standing, sitting, lying down, do not separate from this."

This means that you never leave the Buddhadharma.

> "Once you leave this, you have really missed your chance."

So, in practicing the Dharma, it goes to all the very basic things, like eating, sleeping, and wearing clothes. In these things you have to follow the rules; you can't be confused or casual about it.

> Do not bring forth afflictions;
> Do not bring forth doubt;
> Do not lord it over other people;
> Just consider your own faults.

If you admit that you are wrong,
    and don't contend over principle,
Your natural wisdom will come forth
    in stillness and purity.
Understanding your heart is not a difficult thing,
And perceiving your nature is not bothersome.

The Buddha-light originally pervades
    the Ten Directions,
But our grudges and feuds
    muddle up our minds.
Upon waking up, in a thousand pools
    are a thousand reflections of the moon.
In a cloudless sky, for ten thousand miles
    one can see very clearly.

Man: "How come left-home people are so tied up in seeking fame and profit?"

Abbot: "Their bodies have left home, but their minds and hearts have not yet left home."

Lay people don't have faith in the Sangha because of the Sangha's confused relationships between men and women. That is the cause of the fall of the Dharma in the Orient.

Heng Chau • August 11, 1978
Flatsville!

AARGHH!!!

Convalescing: no appetite, don't want to write or read or sit, no place to go and too weak to travel or attend evening assemblies. I am really frustrated and antsy, like a caged tiger – more intense than *san bu yi bai* – at least I could bow. Now I can't even bow! And I care for nothing. Flatsville!

Heng Sure • August 12, 1978
Day 15 : The treasures are right at home

How many times have I discovered this truth? Most of my afflictions over the past two weeks have to do with not standing up straight.

When my spine is crooked, all my plumbing goes out of line. My
body feels tired, I crash instead of meditating, and my head is
plagued with false thoughts.

I can slump for days on end without recognizing the state. Now,
when I pull it all back into line, I get a great burst of juice and light.
Ah! The Malacca sugar blues melted my spine.

Conversation with the Abbot liberates my heart from an old
shackle. Feels like a mountain stream breaking through a logjam.

Our power is in our youth – our potential for worldly success
and our renunciation of it. We are Westerners, and we reject money,
power, and the good life. We look beyond knowledge and scientific
progress. We are going the other way, riding the vehicle that Asian
Buddhists reject or overlook. We say, "Look at your roots! Your true
treasures are right at home; science has ruined the world; knowledge
and scholarship are worthless."

I read books for eighteen years in all – seven years of college.
Only got confused. Began bowing one word at a time to the sutras.
We have known that academia is false for so long that we don't even
bother to talk about it. We have known for so long that science is
dangerous and stupid that we ignore it.

We see the Buddhadharma with fresh eyes – it is priceless, rare,
true, beneficial to all the world. Bring it back from the scholars, from
the old ladies, from the lay people, from the ash heap, from the
library, from the museum, from the kitchen. Open the sutras. Listen
to the Buddha. Experiment in your own body, in your own heart.
Use your own wisdom to investigate principles. Practice hard. Don't
believe a common viewpoint because it comes from a degree on the
wall. Ph.D.s are a dime a dozen in the West.

Dharma Master Chi Kuang welcomes the Mast

d the delegates to Wonderful Response Temple

"So you can see that Wonderful Response Temp

really getting a wonderful response today…"

A group portrait of the delegation and devote

Wonderful Response Temple, Negeri Sembilan

Heng Chau • August 12, 1978
If you can put down women

The Abbot at lunch the day I fell ill...

"If you can put down women, then you will have no more problems."

Lesson from Malacca:

Whatever or however you seek outside, opens a crack – sooner or later something's going to enter through that crack. Even with cracks, you can protect yourself by being vigorous and careful at all times.

August 13, 1978
Day 16 : Are people afraid of ghosts?

The Abbot's answers to some questions:

Q: "Are there ghosts? Are people afraid of ghosts, or are ghosts afraid of people?"

A: "By your first question, you must have assumed there to be ghosts already, so why bother to ask? As for your second question, when people have ghosts in their minds, then people are afraid of ghosts; when people have no ghosts in their minds, then the ghosts are afraid of people!" (laughter)

Q: "Some people claim that it is not necessary to take refuge in the Triple Jewel and still consider themselves orthodox Buddhists. Is this correct?"

A: "Take studying, for example. If you want to graduate from elementary school, you have to complete the appropriate years in elementary school; if you want to graduate from high school, you have to finish your years of high-school study; the same goes for college, from a B.A., M.A., to Ph.D. degree, you still have to complete the corresponding courses of studies before you can actually graduate... Taking refuge in the Triple Jewel within Buddhism works in this same way."

Q: "Where do people come from?"

A: "Have you seen bugs in grains of rice? Originally there was nothing, then suddenly the bugs appear, as if from nowhere. People arise from true emptiness, according to a similar principle."

The Abbot on food:

"We have been fed so much good food ever since we started, that our delegation has decided to take action. If you continue to feed us so well, we'll have to go on strike. We'll simply not eat. Better still, we have a proposal: just give us simple food. We ask to eat our fill, but not more than that. Rice, bread, only a few vegetable dishes lightly cooked – that's all we request. It hurts us to see so much good food go to waste. Now that I've made this public announcement, I hope you'll help this Dharma Master and keep him from stuffing himself to death."

Heng Sure • August 13, 1978
But they still want to try it out anyway

The Abbot knows that I cannot eat sweet foods. They act on me like alcohol; one mouthful scatters my concentration for hours.

At lunch, three sweet dishes came all at once. With a Chesire-cat grin the Abbot ate a bite, turned to me and asked,

"Would you like some?"

"Is it sweet?"

"Uh huh..."

"No, thanks, I don't dare. A single mouthful wastes an entire day of *gung fu*."

"That serious, is it?"

Then he gestured to the other monks who were spooning it down with vigor. They cluttered and cackled to each other.

"Sweet?"

"Yeah, really!" and made grimaces as the jellied fruit slid down.

"You see," said the Abbot. "They know it's sweet, but they all want to try it out anyway."

The Abbot is teaching and transforming all of the monks and laypeople who draw near him. The lessons are about basic daily Dharma: food, clothes, superstition, vigor. We are all eating lettuce and raw tofu, and all the left-homes are wearing sashes.

Revolution in the Sangha order! Right before our eyes.

I vow in all lives, in all worlds, to propagate, translate, and worship the sutras, the lore, and the images of the great Bodhisattvas, Mahasattvas:

Manjushri Bodhisattva
Samantabhadra Bodhisattva,
Avalokiteshvara Bodhisattva,
Ksitigharba Bodhisattva

To take part in an Earth Store Bodhisattva Dharma Assembly is a moving experience. Earth Store Bodhisattva is a great being. He knows the infinite suffering in the hells and he has promised to stay there and help those who suffer there, helping them to leave.

Until the Hells are empty, I will not become a Buddha.
Only when all beings are saved will I realize Bodhi.

Earth Store Bodhisattva is a hero for all time. His praises must be sung, his vows must be widely known, his story must be told everywhere, his sutra shall be recited and worshipped forever.

As I bowed on stage during the Seremban Earth Store Assembly on Sunday, I found the image of the Bodhisattva totally fascinating. My concentration sharpened; I recited his name as I bowed – time stood still. The image came to life along with the sutra's words that I heard in English, Mandarin, and Cantonese. It was a wonderful state of pure, selfless worship. My heart was deeply moved.

After I sat down the glow continued, and to my joy, the Abbot's face took on the same holy light. He is not different from the greatest of Bodhisattvas.

Heng Sure: "Shih Fu, I got up-tight four days before coming to Gold Mountain and Malaysia."

Abbot: "What were you nervous about?"

Heng Sure: "I wanted to show everyone that I had changed, that cultivation over the last fifteen months had really changed me."

Abbot: "Forget it! Wipe it out! Those fifteen months don't exist! That's just another false thought."

August 14, 1978
Day 17 : Triple Gem Temple – Cameron Highlands

The Abbot's talk on becoming a Buddha:

"First learn to be a real person. Don't learn to be a dog. If you cannot even behave like an upright person, you're too far from being a Buddha. Confucius said,

> A superior person sets up his foundation.
> When the foundation is set up, the Way arises.

The Way is just a method for cultivation; it means shaping a lofty character and establishing virtue.

> Once we learn the way to be human,
> The Buddha's way will be achieved.

"In being a person, there is need to build a firm foundation. Just as when building a skyscraper, we must be sure the ground is very solid. If an individual is likened to a small house, then Buddhism is a huge skyscraper, including all and everything within it.

"Buddhism is just the art of being a person. It means, 'In your words, maintain good faith; in your actions, merit respect.' You have to practice what you preach, and in your actions, start out by respecting yourself. If you do not even respect yourself and do things that cannot face the light, then how can you expect others to respect you? So, in everything you do, do not be casual or sneaky. The Buddha is just a perfected being. He didn't descend from the sky or rise up from the earth. He just cultivated the ten thousand conducts and six paramitas to perfection.

"Why have we not become Buddhas yet? Because we have not seen through everything and put it all down. We haven't even become real people. From now on, you should try to get rid of your selfishness and your attachments to money, sex, fame, food, and sleep. After perfecting the way of a person, you'll attain Buddhahood quite naturally."

Heng Sure • August 14, 1978
The first step is to learn to be a person

Ultra-modern monastery, huge, vacant, gross, and tasteless. Set out among the chalets and resorts of the former colonial ruling class.

Sense of rotting foundations… masquerade – like a movie-set to be discarded after the last take. It is a ghostly place. Surrounded by ghosts and energy-hungry demons. Tea-table piled with ten varieties of sugar cakes, loud voices, emotional juice gushing, sharp commands, slow responses. Flies everywhere.

"Our group must always sit together, wherever we go we sit as a group," directs the Abbot. For self-defense clearly.

And then a change. After the Abbot's Dharma-talk, the people all transformed into family. Bright-eyed, laughing and relaxed. They took refuge with joyful faces and the darkness was dispelled.

Heng Sure: "You know, my biggest problem is not being able to sit Ch'an."

Abbot: "Make time in the middle of the chaos. Anyway you needn't necessarily sit in order to cultivate. You can use effort wherever you are.

"Cultivating the hands is just like eating. You may not seek a result. You don't eat with the thought that this bite is going here and nourishing this and that and winding up as excrement. This is all false thought. You just eat. Cultivation is the same way. You simply do it without expecting results.

"The first step to Buddhahood is to learn to be a person. The fundamental condition for being a person is to secure your foundation in principle: filiality to your parents and obedience to your teachers and elders.

"In order to be a person, speak earnestly and with truth. Respect yourself. Don't look down on what you do. Don't preserve a pessimistic attitude towards your self. If you slight yourself and do cheap, lazy, unworthy things, then there will be many things that you cannot accomplish!"

Abbot: "These two are *san bu yi bai* – eight-hundred miles. They go one mile a day. They are really sincere. Their magical responses have been incredible. When it rains cats and dogs, for a mile around them it doesn't rain."

Abbot Ben Tao: "This is the Master's doing."

Abbot: "It's because they aren't lazy for even one minute. They work hard day and night. I'm really happy with them.

"I invite you to come to the City of Ten Thousand Buddhas. It's a place for cultivation. You can enter seclusion there. Dharma Master Seng is thinking of doing just that. You should come and be a model for all these young people."

Abbot Ben Tao: "The Abbot is a pioneer, opening up the West. He is Guan Shi Yin Bodhisattva. He is Earth Store Bodhisattva. His eyebrows are really long."

Heng Chau • August 14, 1978
These Americans aren't dumb cookies

Cameron Highlands for lunch: Monday.

Ribbing at meal from Shih Fu about sickness caused by false-thoughts about women:

"No one else knew, but I knew. If I couldn't read their minds, they (Americans) would have all left long ago. These Americans aren't dumb cookies.

"Kuo T'ung acted out his impulses to chase women physically. Kuo T'ing did it in his mind, but it was the same thing. Thinking good, not thinking bad, then you are able to see your original face before your parents bore you."

August 15, 1978
Day 18 : Purple Bamboo Grove temple – Ipoh, Perak

The Abbot speaks about the disunity within Buddhism:

"I have disciples who are as stupid as myself, and they do not know how to say pleasant things. I am this way too, yet I want to speak the truth. What is it? The greatest problem within Buddhism right now is selfishness and self-seeking. Sects pit themselves against sects, temples against temples, and Dharma masters against Dharma masters. What was originally a perfect religion is divided up by political factions, much hatred, and small-mindedness. If we cannot unite ourselves within Buddhism, there is even less chance that we can be open to other religions of the world. This is the space age, but why boast about travel to other stars and galaxies when we haven't even straightened out our own planet? Why should left-home people be greedy for money and offerings? Haven't we left home just to transcend the three realms? If we like money so much, we needn't leave home. There are plenty of money-earning occupations in lay life."

The Abbot's continues in the afternoon:

"Left-home people should see through such things as money and fame. Why should left-home people hoard a lot of money anyway? Therefore, I urge – if we are at all intent upon reforming the Dharma – that Sanghans give up holding private assets under their own names. They should give them to the Central Assembly. Take, for example, the Catholics: the central government is in the Vatican, and all the legislation and resources are controlled there by a central committee. Priests everywhere do not keep private assets. They receive a given allowance per month for their needs, but they do not dabble in business. They probably have realized the trouble that money can get one into. If you don't have money, you keep on cultivating; but once you have money your head gets turned. The reason this is called the Dharma Ending Age is precisely because people have forgotten to cultivate. They are bound by the chains of the five desires.

"In Buddhism, what we lack most is healthy educational institutions. Without schools and dissemination of Buddhist principles, how can people recognize Buddhism for its true worth? Will people respect us if we are immersed in external show and superstitions? For this reason I have vowed to translate the holy sutras into all the languages of the world. This is a project of immense scale and probably requires the backing of the government in order to be truly feasible. Yet, we have started from nothing. From 1968 until the present, the International Institute for the Translation of Buddhist Texts has translated thirty volumes of the sutras. Dharma Realm Buddhist University and the City of Ten Thousand Buddhas arose as a direct response to the need of our present time. The City of Ten Thousand Buddhas simply sprang forth from the earth, because the time is ripe.

"I've decided to dedicate the City to the entire world – to Buddhists of the entire world and to people of other religions as well. Buddhism has begun afresh in America. I have vowed that wherever I go, I'll only allow the Proper Dharma to thrive.

"Now America is a leader among the countries of the world, and if Buddhism catches on there, other countries will be influenced, provided we practice the true Dharma. I am giving the City of Ten Thousand Buddhas as the headquarters of World Buddhism, a place where Buddhists from all countries, and people of other religions as well, can come to study and cultivate in harmony. Next year, in the fall, there will be a grand opening ceremony of the City of Ten Thousand Buddhas and Dharma Realm Buddhist University. We will hold an International Convention of Buddhism, during which time we will elect a world leader of Buddhism. We've been too long without any organization, without any focus. In order to be strong again, we need a central government. The solution to our critical situation is to be without selfishness. If we put down our own attachments to money and fame, and give ourselves up solely to the thriving of Buddhism, there is no doubt that our religion will spread to every corner throughout all of empty space."

Heng Sure • August 15, 1978
Your 112 is no problem

I got scolded when I gave my responsibility for making decisions about my work over to the Abbot again. I returned to an old bad habit of seeking his approval from a subservient position; putting him into a position of authority that he doesn't take.

His message:

Strike up your spirits!
Stand on your own!
Don't rely on others!

If I am sincere, a way will open up. Seek neither praise nor censure from others. Do not fear disapproval. There will always be those who like the worst people and who dislike the best people.

I must be absolutely straight when I talk. Inside humble, outside reverent. Be unafraid. Sweep away politeness, style, form, rules. All are outer appearances which obstruct the truth that connects hearts.

The phoney formality is oppressive.

Abbot: "I was really skinny when I was cultivating, too. Only after I got to Hong Kong did I get heavier. Heaviest I was 160, most comfortable about 130, but then I am a little fuller than you – heavier all round, so your 112 is no problem.

"Forget it! How can your appearance obstruct the Proper Dharma. Who pays attention to this? Just be sincere."

Heng Chau • August 15, 1978
The inner trip through Asia

Ride to Ipoh.

Looking at women with desire is a habit. The same kind of habit energy as good clothes, false speech, overeating, being late, etc. It can be changed. The thought behind it is ignorance – fear of no self leads to grasping at existence. Soon the thought produces its own energy and a habit develops. Sexual desire is a habit. Recognize the cause and root it out. At the same time, replace and monitor the habit which now has a life of its own. Interesting – how much of what I think, say, and do is rooted in greed, hatred, and stupidity. Just basic ignorance at the beginning, and in the end, one is off a thousand miles. "Everything is a question of habit," says the Abbot.

At first, my response was fear and resistance – deep and almost unconscious. Travelling in Asia is acting as a catalyst for the real journey – the inner trip – away from all attachments and free of false thoughts. A foreign land, foreign tongue, and foreign faces – nothing familiar or predictable. The Abbot's *dz dzai* (self mastery) is the touchstone and a source of courage and vigor.

Heng Sure • August 16, 1978
Day 19 : Tung Lien Siao Tzu

A transition came at Seremban. After lunch at a layman's house and a long ride to Seremban, Wonderful Response Temple, I realized my heart's wish to give the Dharma to our group, to all beings, and felt a big opening – taking charge of my self and my work, helping out.

At once Shih Fu gave me the chance to speak by having me introduce the group. He then put me in charge of Kuo T'ung and Heng Ch'au.

I went too far with it – it was not a license to talk. There is enough responsibility in this job to occupy my full attention. Don't talk! That is blowing the seals! Keep the rules. Don't be turned.

Heng Chau • August 16, 1978
Five-and-ten-cent special

What happened to my energy and *chi?* I've never felt so low-fire and hard-to-start. I feel like I'm half submerged, or wearing lead swimming trunks. The heat? Ego tricks? A test? I don't know, but it feels like someone switched my battery and left me with a half-charged five-and-ten-cent special.

August 17, 1978
Day 20 : Roam playfully in the world

The Abbot's instructions in the morning:

"Never be nervous. Always keep a light and easy mind, in everything be happy. See all things as transformations, bubbles, dewdrops, and illusions. All is false. Roam playfully in the world; just try your best. We are born into the world to pay back old debts."

A girl from the temple asks the Abbot:

"Should I leave home or stay at home – which is a better way to cultivate?"

"If you can put everything down, it is better to leave home."

"But, I still have an old mother to take care of."

"Then you still cannot put everything down."

At the Laymen's Association, the Abbot talks about his mission to the West:

"I have come to create Buddhas, Bodhisattvas, patriarchs, and arhats. I am an artisan, but I do not work with gold, stone, clay, or wood. Rather, I prefer to create living Buddhas, living Bodhisattvas, living patriarchs, and living arhats from living flesh. Everybody who comes to cultivate at the City of Ten Thousand Buddhas must become a Buddha!"

Heng Sure • August 17, 1978
Opening my mouth is not okay

Opening my mouth is not okay. All systems fail when I leak this light. Sincerely bow. Open your heart. Observe. Contemplate. Stand straight and mind your own business.

Heng Chau • August 17, 1978
Sacrificed peanuts

I have only vaguely recognized what has been happening inside – a continuation of the *san bu yi bai* breakdown, only intensified by the Abbot's closeness and the Asia trip.

Yesterday I was right up against the emptiness of dharmas and myself. How much patience could I muster to wait out this state and see what was on the other side of it? Fighting the sleep demon and fatigue and the "can't-raise-my-spirits" ghost.

Night bowing was unbearable; I felt anger and impatience with the lecture, the heat, the crowd. Really hard to face and overcome when it's for real. Inertia and ego-resistance is powerful and hard to recognize.

Abbot: "When you get to the point of death, just keep going like always."

Where will the strength come from this time? If I don't use effort, what then?

The arena has become small and boring – food is flat and uninteresting, clothes and sleep the same. My women outflow has been exposed and lost its power. All that's left is bowing and facing the demons. Really hard!

And yet, compared to the ancients, I've sacrificed peanuts in my search for the Way. What a poor showing for a disciple who is given so much by his teacher!

Born from womb, leave home, accomplish the Way, and speak the Dharma.

Heng Sure • August 18, 1978
Day 21 : Setiawan, Perak

A two-story garage; no running water – Malaysian rural Chinese. The Abbot's patience is unshakable. He gets no rest, he wants none. He babysits us, waiting for us to break free of the old, dirty habits and become Buddhists.

Heng Chau • August 18, 1978
Suffering and impermanence

Impermanence! In the last week, the whole world and myself have gone empty before my eyes. There's something about life in Asia – it's up close and out in front. The heat and poverty brings people and life's conditions face-to-face out in the streets. Old age, birth, sickness, and death are ever present. It pounds on the eyes, ears, nose, tongue, body, and mind. Suffering and impermanence isn't glossed over and prettied up – it's raw. All beings are in this world of suffering and impermanence – I am, too.

People in their 20-40's, with families, jobs – burdened and worried about money, bills, growing kids. Old people, wrinkled and slow, with bodies failing and going bad. They watch and wait. Their faces show the struggle and hassle of dragging around tired skin bags and being in the way and unwanted. Birth, dwelling, decay, and emptiness interpenetrate and fuse people, animals, houses, and plants. The Wheel of Life, the six paths of rebirth, chews up living beings and spits them out again and again. What joy is there in this!?

Upasaka Kuo K'ung: "That's kind of my philosophy. I just try my best and then let things happen naturally and don't get caught up in feelings and a lot of emotion."

One of the points of cultivation is to expand the measure of your mind – to get rid of pettiness and small thinking and focus on the essentials. Find what unites and touches all living beings and throw out the things that divide and isolate us. What is it we all share?

"The teaching of all living beings." This is the Buddhadharma – just the raw basics. Get rid of the discriminating mind and merge with the whole. Bring forth a single heart, a single body. Self is false.

Heng Sure • August 19, 1978
Day 22 : Taiping

I want to do it, to qualify. To purify the last, utmost edge of my being. It has to happen. I feel myself on the edge of the cliff, committed to leaping off into the deepest water. Slow-motion entry, strong resistance. Go! No. Wait!

The slow change is in recognizing who I am. Isolating the faults and impurities and washing them clean. Slow grinding, polishing. None of it has to do with thought.

Finding the habit. Recognizing it as I take it on.

Taiping Buddhist Association
August, 1978

Heng Chau • August 19, 1978
Internal purging and smelting

I am going through heavy and internal purging and smelting. Can never seem to get over the top of an energy sag. Eating is the delicate balance – too little, and no fuel; too much causes fire and diarrhea. Each city is different and often it's trial and error day-to-day.

I don't recognize states clearly. The whole karmic process is rich with contours and subtle crevices – steep and deceptive. The patience required blows my mind, and I fail miserably with my impatience and shortsightedness.

Heng Sure • August 20, 1978
Day 23 : It used to be my parents and teachers

"This is your responsibility. Your life is your own, moving from thought to thought. Nothing is fixed. Work on your own. Try your best."

This is the hardest thing to face. Taking charge of cause and effect, owning my troubles and my ghosts. I still harbor the view that it's okay to sneak around my own rules, as long as "the authorities" don't catch me. It used to be my parents and teachers – now it's the Abbot. I give him the role of cop and take for myself the job of naughty child – less than before, but I still do it.

His response: patience, subtle expedients to let me know he's watching my thoughts and waiting for me to work it out.

At the same time, I go yinny and give over my sense of self-approval. He completely ignores me – speaks to others in a low voice in my presence so that I have to commit the effort to listen in or else admit that my job is to keep bowing and stop seeking approval.

There is always the feeling of a carrot dangling just in front of this donkey's nose.

We're on the equator in the hottest time of the year. Repeatedly we have requested the hosts in each town we visit to prepare foods without oil or frying or sugar, and each lunch table is regularly piled high with fried, oily, sweet foods – most of them return to the kitchen uneaten. We all go hungry nearly every day – our bodies simply cannot endure the fire in the food that we are served. It is a never-ending battle.

Heng Chau • August 20, 1978
Your merit and virtue ran away

About a hundred sincere people do *san bu yi bai* around a Bodhi tree in front of the Taiping Temple. Some are old and feeble – one woman with no toes and barely enough breath, but she kept at it. All without words or language – everyone knew.

Realizations.

"Your merit and virtue ran away. But don't worry, it will come back." (Hoeh Beng)

"Your false thoughts about women almost killed you. You lost it, but you can build it up again." (Taiping)

Nodding, hunger, no stamina or reserve strength. *Yin* states of doubt, fear, low resolve. Why? I was sicker than I realized. If it hadn't been for the Abbot, I'd be dead now. During the two critical days, he always came to my bed at the key moments with a head rub, mantras, and/or hand movements along with humor and kind words. "I brought you back from King Yama this time. Hurry up and die." Some debts cannot be measured or repaid.

I've never felt so wasted and drained. I lost a lot. Hard to say how much – it feels like everything but a few embers.

Another realization.

My *mau bing* is desire, seeking. At core it's women, female recognition and ego attachment to a woman's presence. At the fringe it manifests as seeking fame, food, sleep, success, e.g., university career, etc. – all #1's, parent pleasers, the emperor. "Ignorance conditions action."

Abbot: "Maybe I'll come to your cave and hang out for a while." (to a monk)

Kuo K'ung: "Shih Fu, you couldn't do that! We have a full and tight schedule…"

Abbot: "I can put it all down at any time."

He is completely happy within emptiness that isn't empty. Shih Fu is kind – he monitors our needs and our greed and by using various means gives us enough time to eat without overdoing, if we chose to follow his lead. Today he handed me a plate of tomatoes and raw cauliflower as the meal began. Message: eat this. Stay out of the other food.

Sexual desire is pure ignorance – selfish and dark. It obstructs our entry into the Buddhadharma like the walls of a narrow cave as we grope to find the bright sun. We emerge into boundless, empty space, glowing and free, once we see through our attachments to the body and its sexual function. This is the root of birth and death.

August 21, 1978
Day 24 : Buddhist Association – Penang

At night the Abbot lectures about the precept sash in front of about two thousand people:

"Most left-home people have totally lost track of the significance of wearing their precept sashes. Many go around in their long robes with large butterfly sleeves, thinking this will suffice. This long robe is but a traditional costume handed down from the T'ang dynasty, a robe that laypeople also wore. Even in Japan now they wear robes like this. By no means does wearing this long-sleeved robe classify you as a left-home person. Only your sash does. The Buddha admonished his disciples to wear the precept sash in order to manifest the appearance of a Bhikshu. If you run around in your long robe or short shirt-and-pants outfit, you are no different from a layperson. All the Theravadan monks constantly wear their sashes. That is why people pay them respect. Yet we of the Mahayana tradition have forgotten to wear ours over the centuries, to the point that now wearing the precept sash is considered outlandish. Wouldn't you say this is upside-down?

"Originally the monks in China wore sashes too. But the winters in China were harsh, and people had to wear clothes underneath their sashes. These sashes which were made of silky material, slipped off easily, and many of them were lost. Now, left-home people could not afford to lose so many sashes, so they had a conference during the T'ang dynasty. This is a recording from their meeting at the T'ang dynasty. They didn't have tape-recorders then, so don't ask me how I know. Anyway, a Patriarch came up with a suggestion. 'Why not sew a hook on one end of the sash and a clasp on the other? With the clasp fastened to the hook, our sashes would not slip off.' Everybody thought it a peerless idea, and from that time all adopted the hook-and-clasp tradition. Still, people had to work, and during menial labor they found it very inconvenient to wear their sashes. They started taking them off, and bit by bit, sashes were only retained for ceremonies. Left-home people became more and more lax about the habit, so that down through the dynasties – T'ang, Sung, Yuan, Ming, and Ch'ing – people eventually forsook the habit of wearing sashes altogether. Now it is considered an eyesore to be wearing sashes.

"That is why some people call us 'weird' in America because the left-home people there wear their sashes all the time. We are just doing what we were supposed to do all along. Just consider the verse,

> Fine indeed, this robe of liberation.
> Unsurpassed sash, the field of blessings.
> I now most respectfully don it,
> And hope to wear it lifetime after lifetime.

If you hope to wear it 'lifetime after lifetime,' shouldn't it be a case of wearing it 'moment after moment' as well?"

The Abbot on affinities:

"All of you young and old friends, my masters and my disciples, we've been together since beginningless time and still do not recognize one another. Why is this? It's because we've been too confused, too covered over by ignorance, that we've turned around and around without cease."

Heng Sure • August 21, 1978
Still hungry with too many bananas

Another skirmish – it is hard to win. I'm still hungry, but my belly is bloated with too many bananas. My head is full of fire from the raunchy food. Sugar and oil everywhere – the "special vegetable plate" is covered with sugary salad dressing, the tofu is an oily soup, the rice stops coming when the other Dharma Masters are through. They eat three meals a day, so they finish quickly and watch as we scarf down what we can find that's clean to eat.

August 22, 1978
Day 25 : Do you think they are easy to subdue?

The Abbot on temples:

"Some people build temples and forget to build cultivators. I also am a temple builder, a bricklayer, yet I request living Buddhas to dwell inside my temples."

The Abbot on desires:

"I am one without a bit of sexual desire. You can put any beautiful girl in front of me and my mind will not move. If it were not for this total lack of desire, do you think Americans would buy what I have to teach them? Do you think these Americans are easy to subdue?

"As for the other desires: I've seen a lot of money come and go, but I myself am not greedy for it. As for fame, what's the difference between a good and bad name? If I cared about fame, would I call myself an ant, a mosquito, a horse? As for food, everything I eat is of one flavor to me. Finally sleep, I can go on several nights without sleep, and then I can also doze off for several months... Isn't this wonderful?" (cheers and applause)

Heng Sure • August 22, 1978
Taking refuge with lunch

Eye-opening experience: a round of temples in Penang.

Venerable Chu Mo runs a clean Buddhist School. Dharma-heir of Venerable Tai Hsu, his Earth Store statue is powerful, the rooms full of beads, books, trinkets, instruments.

Guan Yin Temple – the Dharma-ending Age tour. Fried ducks and chickens on the main altar. "Monks here are counterfeit, not for real," says a layman. "They have thirty or forty wives." We don't even stop to bow. There's a sense of deviant, ugly decay.

Ji Le Ssu (Garden of Ultimate Bliss) – Dark, heavy vibes. The Abbot proceeds to teach and transform all present. A feeling of old sickness being dispelled. The two chief monks confess that they have done nothing within the Dharma since leaving home. The Abbot instructs them, invites them to the City of Ten Thousand Buddhas. They all acknowledge his patriarchate from the Elder Hsu Yun. The Abbot's light purifies and heals all hearts. The monks seek it like eager novices – each looks thirty years younger.

Myau Hsiang Ling (Grove of Wonderful Fragrance) –

D.M. Kuang Yu: "My hair has turned white for the sake of this place."

Found a *san bu yi bai* bowing space in my head today for the first time since the trip began. Quiet and still.

Afflictions afterward – hot, seeking, and uptight. About what? Food! Hungry and looking forward to tomorrow's meal. This is an old familiar trap called taking refuge in lunch. The way to turn it is to eat Dharma, to sit long and let the desire fall away like layers of onion skin.

Heng Chau • August 22, 1978
Where are the young Bhikshus?

Bowing at Penang.

More clearly than ever, I'm coming to see my *mau bing* – the need to be noticed, looked up to, admired, recognized, the center and #1, etc. And yet, all my life this urge was at odds with the one who sought stillness and ultimate wisdom, the one who wanted the true and the oneness of being alone. Now I have the chance (in fact, I've always had the chance), but I still can't put it down in my heart clearly. How paradoxical! Anonymity – no longer "bigs." Do I fear that so much that I am willing to kill myself before I'd let go of that false attachment?

Specific: the pet of all the girls, everybody's kid brother and animus, cute and lots of personality. Now, to really turn that light around is the heart of my Dharma. And yet, I piddle around at it like I am immortal!

The Abbot: "Don't stop, strive onward, don't ever be satisfied with yourself. The time is nearly right to collect all of the assets of Buddhism in the world together at the City of Ten Thousand Buddhas."

Myau Hsiang Lin is adorned with Italian marble, Italian porcelain, Buddha-images that resemble Madonnas, and mosaic phoenixes and dragons on all sides made from shards of ceramic cups. Here is a sense of self-indulgent waste of resources.

"I've got all this, and it's mine," says Dharma Master Kuang Yu.

"I've got the City of Ten Thousand Buddhas, and I don't care to keep even a hair of it for myself," says the Abbot. "These Americans are not stupid, they respect me only because I am not in the least selfish. Every penny that comes in goes to the general fund. No one keeps any offerings as private capital. This place is nice, but we will have a bigger scope at the City of Ten Thousand Buddhas. Our minds must expand to include the whole world, not just China.

"We eat one meal a day. No breakfast. Most people can't bear it. That's the way we do it. Most people say that in the Dharma-ending Age it is wrong to endure bitterness, that we should enjoy pleasure instead. I say that the Dharma's end is in your heart. If you uphold what's proper, it's the Proper Dharma Age."

* * *

I have rebalanced my body for hot weather. It is time to return to balanced eating. No more gobbling. No more desire and stuffing. Don't be selfish at the table. Dirty eating = dirty vessel.

What a huge mistake it would be to step off center for as long as an instant seeking anything. Tempted to try for a copy of the Buddhist terms list book. To do so would have cashed in our group's blessings totally. Bitter and cheap. Sit back. If it's in your path, it will come to you.

People are all watching me eat and drink to see if I am true and real. Don't seek anything. Serve all Buddhist disciples. Any place you can give up yourself – even a little bit – for others, do it gladly, with vigor. This is the real prize.

"In general, as long as you still have a self, you can't do anything. The Bodhisattva does nothing that benefits himself; he strives to serve others." (the Abbot)

* * *

The '56 Plymouth looks so good compared to these ornamental mansions. The pure, straight mind is the Bodhimanda. Simple, reverent, humble, bitter, filled with spirit is the Way. Clean and free.

Hundreds of thousands of dollars have been spent for imported Italian ornaments in this temple – costly ceramic mosaic gargoyles on the roofs – no young monks in sight – empty, silent temples.

Where are the young Bhikshus in Malaysia? Who will carry out the patriarchs' pulse when the over-50 generation is gone? How will the Proper Dharma survive without a vigorous Sangha?

Every monk has a castle and a flock of laypeople. Some keep the rules and the practices, some don't. Who cares? Who checks?

With so few men studying the Dharma and fewer still practicing it, each unsung ceremony, each abandoned ritual and practice brings the Dharma closer to extinction. Soon no one will remember.

Watching Yu Kuo K'ung's wisdom open like a flower under the Abbot's sunshine. This is Kuo Kung's hour. His speaking improves by the day. It is encouraging. What keeps me from being free? My false thoughts and attachments. Otherwise, I could be liberated right here, right now in Malaysia with the Abbot just inches away. But you are still bound up in self, still dreaming.

Kuo Chen, go for the heart of it. Drop the false frills, the useless externals. There is no time for the superficial aspects. There are too few people who know the true from the false. Your job is to uncover the essence, protect the seed, and bring it to the West.

* * *

My faith and vigor are really being tested. And, under the circumstances, the one-meal-a-day is really bitter and hard to get by on. The ginseng is an expedient life-saver. I can't drink the milk-sugar drinks that abound – they're pure desire.

I've got the okay from the Abbot to get out of my *hu fa* role while in Asia – no cooking, no talking to women, etc. "You can just use single-minded effort at cultivation."

Seclusion.

"Most people go into seclusion and then write letters all over the world," says the Abbot.

"He's not emperor anymore; he dropped his title as emperor. Now he's just a shramanera (novice). Really arrogant – he wouldn't even *kow tow* (bow) at first."

Heng Sure • 23 August, 1978
Day 26 : Attacked by mad yins

Attacked and subdued by the mad yins. It could be something simple, like not taking a shower for too long. Keeping the bowing heat feels like a mistake – it should be released at night.

Or it could just be the Pisces blues. Or no fire fuel at lunch. Maybe I lack enough fire?

Something took all my energy, concentration, and spirits – I feel like a zombie, lost in a cloud of yinny despair.

August 24, 1978
Day 27 : Butterworth, Penang

On the Central Welcoming Committee's arrangements of sociable visits to local chief monks, temples, press and other groups, the Abbot announces:

"Who do you think I am? I am not any Dharma master who has come from abroad to socialize. I stated very clearly in my letters before I arrived that I do not go visiting, I do not attend social lunches, and I do not throw social banquets.

"We are left-home people. If we do this, what difference is there between us and the laypeople of the world? How can we act in a corrupt manner? We leave home to cultivate a world-transcending dharma. If we want to swim around in the mud, why leave home at all?

"Our delegates all have important work to do. Not one single moment is spared. Don't think that we sit in our rooms taking a snooze. Don't judge us by your own standards."

The Abbot to a few young people:

"You are young and vigorous; you should be on my side instead of listening to the rattle of old antiques. We should change whatever customs that are not in accord with Dharma. They've gone down the wrong path; do you expect me to swim in the filth with them? Buddhism is pure; we should restore it to its original purity by guarding over our every act."

Heng Sure • August 24, 1978
Who am I – talking in Chinese?

Two monks whom I embarrassed with my dietary demands share our table. I go ahead and eat things that I refused at their temple. Crude and rude. They are so boggled by Americans that they may just overlook it.

Butterworth Temple, Penang

Talking to young people in Butterworth, a family temple full of decaying Dharma. Their faces were bright, doubtful about monks, but excited by our new blood.

Who am I – talking in Chinese, wearing a false smile, quoting my teacher's words, then re-interpreting my behavior to my friends in American terms?

I found it easier to do than if I had to speak English to college students for two hours where I would have to speak from my heart.

I've found rich resources of Chinese language Buddhadharma at my fingertips. Did it bypass my heart? Who is Heng Sure, that he can be false but fears being true? Why am I stumped by this last obstacle of self? I can put down everything but my fears and afflictions.

I can put food down – milk and sugar, flavor – I can cut them off. At a stage of gradual starvation my teacher told me to ease back on to the middle path. Intentional hunger is an attachment to a state. Desire must be overcome in the heart, not just subdued in the body. I hold on to my fear and bad habits as if they were my armor in a battlefield.

Heng Chau • August 24, 1978
The old sickness that I can't put down

As soon as I get a little light, my mouth opens and I spill it out. When will I learn? I was just starting to regather it all within the last two days and was really getting filled by the Abbot, and then I shot it out in a tête-à-tête with Heng Sure after lunch and in the car with Kuo T'ung and Heng Sure on the way to the temple in Butterfield... stupid!

Holding forth, rapping on, playing counselor-king – not recognizing the same old pattern I've been struggling with since meeting the Abbot. This "old *mau bing*" that I can't put down. It's seeking and leaking, but I make it seem like giving. I give because I'll get.

Seeking to be #1 – the emperor – is right where the problem is. It's natural; I vow to reverse it.

Heng Ch'au: "Shih Fu, is it that the hexes and sorcerers and people who try to disrupt the assemblies are just different manifestations of the same energy?"

Abbot: "You could say that."

Politics and Buddhism, energy of good and evil on a large and small scale, is starting to become clear to me on this trip. It's all made from the mind. All good or bad energy begins there and ends there. The problem or solution is just us, not parties or religions or ideologies. Greed, anger, stupidity – or morality, compliance, and wisdom. It never goes beyond this. All of the possibilities and potentials in the entire universe (Dharma Realm) is within the heart of each living being, and "not beyond a single thought."

All dharmas return to the same source, but Ch'an is the highest and hardest and most direct.

August 25, 1978
Day 28 : Penang Buddhist Association

The Abbot on the precept sash:

"As time went on, monks just found it too 'inconvenient' to wear sashes and finally gave them up altogether. Nowadays the reverse of what is proper is in vogue. You're considered an odd-ball if you wear your sash."

The Abbot talks about the present state of Buddhism in the world in front of a group of two hundred youngsters:

"In Buddhism we each set up our own factions and parties; you say you're fine, I say I'm fine. Nobody is willing to admit that he is an imperfect Buddhist disciple. Instead we indulge in backbiting and gossiping.

"Mahayana monks call themselves Bodhisattvas, yet most of them do not even put on their precept sashes. Theravadans claim that the Mahayana faith isn't even Buddhism. If we maintain such strife within Buddhism itself, just imagine the flack we give to other religions. The Buddha did not teach us to be so petty and narrow-minded. Rather, we should include every living being in the entirety of empty space and the Dharma Realm – whether they believe or not – within Buddhism. The Buddha said, 'All living beings have the Buddhanature, all can become Buddhas.' Hence, even if a living being does not believe in the Buddha, he still has an inherent Buddhanature, so how can we exclude him from Buddhism? Unless one can run outside of empty space and the Dharma Realm, one cannot run outside of Buddhism. Whether he believes or not is just a matter of time. If you do not believe in Buddhism this lifetime, I'll wait for you until your next life, and on and on – even for measure-less kalpas – I will still wait for you.

"If we expand the measure of our hearts, then all human beings can unite and benefit the world. For the rise and fall of a country, every person bears a responsibility. As for the rise and fall of Buddhism, every Buddhist disciple should take it as his own responsibility, too. Do not bow to the Buddhas merely out of greed for wealth and fame; rather offer up good conduct and be a true disciple. We at the City of Ten Thousand Buddhas and Dharma Realm Buddhist University aim at grooming young people to get rid of their greed, anger, and selfishness, so that they can mold a new and better world. I hope one day all of you will come to study at the City of Ten Thousand Buddhas."

A question and answer session follows after the talk:

Q: "Amitabha Buddha teaches us to recite his name and promises us rebirth with our karmic load in the Land of Ultimate Bliss. Yet, in Buddhist theory it is maintained that we can realize Buddhahood only through our own effort. Isn't this a contradiction?"

A: "When you recite Namo Amitabha, it's not that you just daydream and recite sporadically. You have to recite sincerely to a point of single-mindedness in order to get a response. When you reach that point, you do not know whether it is you or the Buddha who is reciting. You ask me whether you are relying on the Buddha to be reborn in the Western world. I feel it is by your own effort that you get there."

Q: "You say that in order to cultivate and end birth and death we have to cut off desire. What is meant by that, and how does one cut off desire?"

A: "What is your motive for asking this question? If you do not want to cut off desire, why bother to ask? Do you think this is just a joke?

"You don't want to cut off desire, you can't put it down, so why bother? Do you think cutting off desire is as easy as asking the question? Not to speak of you – a layperson – how many old monks haven't cut it off!

"So you think it only takes asking a question to cut off desire. You aren't even qualified to ask! First you haven't left home, and that is the number-one prerequisite which you have not fulfilled. Besides, you don't really want to put it down."

Q: "Is there such a thing as fate; what is the relationship between fate and causes and conditions?"

A: "Some people believe in predestination, and there's nothing much you can do to convince them otherwise. However,

A superior person realizes that he is creating his own destiny. Our fate is determined by us; we seek our own blessings. Disasters and blessings have no door; we ourselves search for ways to enter into them. The rewards for doing good and the retributions for doing evil follow us like a shadow.

"You can forge your own destiny. If everything depended on fate, then even with regard to becoming a Buddha or not, you'd have to consult a fortune teller."

The Abbot at Universiti Sains Malaysia:

"All of you are smart people with promise. The ten-thousand things are all speaking Dharma. Desks speak desk-dharma, chairs speak chair-dharma. Last night there was a question as to how the Dharma wheel is turned; actually, people turn the people-dharma wheel, dogs turn the dog-dharma wheel, and cats turn the cat-dharma wheel. If you understand, then the Dharma you hear is one of wisdom. If you do not understand, the dharma you hear will be one of stupidity. These are very simple words, but if you truly carry them with you, they will be worth a lifetime's use. If you understand, you will no longer do upside-down things, be turned by money and fame, and upon death go wailing with empty hands.

"Do not wait till old age to study the Way; the lonely graves are full of young people. Make good use of your youth and your intelligence; do not follow the example of old antiques, because your ancestors may not have done everything right.

"Some people claim that Buddhism has to adhere strictly to tradition, like insisting on long robes with large sleeves, which are a carry-over from the Han Dynasty. Now, I happen to think that in this day and age where material is scanty, this is a real waste of resources. Here we are parading around with these clumsy sleeves, and in other places people don't even have any clothes to wear. It is too impractical, too unfair.

"There's another custom I'd like to change: the habit of throwing large banquets amongst Sanghans, particularly for visiting Dharma masters. People like to cook up a storm for their guests. I've eaten so much food recently that I do not know whether I am a pig, a dog, or a person. 'One banquet at a rich man's house: half a year of rations in a poor man's home.' From childhood I was poor, so when I see so much good food go to waste, it really pains my heart. I've stuck to my principle of not visiting and not throwing banquets. It wastes too much time – coming back and forth – the time can be put to much better use.

"When I touched down at Taiwan a few years ago, the first thing I said to the people who greeted me at the airport was, 'I'm not going out on any lunches and visiting tours, even if the President were to invite me, I'd still not go.' I simply don't have a thousand hundred billion transformation bodies. At Seremban, the food was so good that we were forced to take action. Our group announced that we would go on strike, that we would not eat, if this continued. Then they quickly adjusted our menus. Now we have much simpler and more edible food. We are left-home people; we are well aware of the limit of our blessings and do not want to exhaust them."

Heng Sure • August 25, 1978
Just like a Chinese

Lunch at the Malaysian Buddhist Association.

In conversation with D.M. Bai Sheng, the Abbot's attitude was disarming, kind, and friendly.

Abbot: "You came? You're not afraid of me after all? Don't worry. I won't scold you – I've changed.

"All Sangha members should make their assets public property. My place is the biggest, so as to set a good example I'm the first one to pitch into the kitty. I'm a revolutionary within the Sangha, don't you know? I support wearing the sash and getting rid of the *hai ching* robe.

"Four U.S. shramaneras pitched food out of the window at the precept ceremony in Taiwan."

Bai Sheng: "I didn't know."

Abbot: "Of course you didn't. An overseas delegation came to San Francisco and whooped it up, stepped out on the town, and broke all the precepts."

D.M. Kuo Jing: "You two ate so little…?" (bating)

D.M. Ju Mwo: "Well, we eat three meals a day."

Eating one meal a day was defended. The reasons for silence at the table were explained to D.M. Ru Chien by D.M. Kuo Jing. We were all likened to Chinese people.

Two monks: "They all look a little Chinese."

Abbot: "Sure, that's because they all were/are Chinese."

My silence was explained, and then when I picked up every grain of rice that I had spilled around my bowl, D.M. Ru Chien said,

"Inconceivable – that this American has been transformed. He cleans up every last bite of food, just like a Chinese."

The Abbot beamed. Big score today.

August 26, 1978
Day 29 : Bukit Mertajam – Penang

The Abbot gives some words of encouragement to youths:

"You are a youth organization. This implies that you shouldn't follow blindly the stupid examples that some old people set up, but rely on your own discriminating wisdom. Always wield your Jeweled Pestle, so that at all moments you can subdue demons and external ways. Now, this vajra pestle is not visible, it exists inside your mind. Your mind has to be firm, you should be patient, and never fight or argue. Discriminate between right and wrong. If it accords with the Way, progress; if it is counter to the Way, retreat from it. Do not use force. Why not? Once you use force, you're no longer compassionate. Note how wars begin: because of greed and selfishness. I do not protest against wars. Young people protest, but this is just fighting fire with fire. As soon as this war is done with, another one will flare up somewhere else. You haven't gotten to the root of the problem. Rather, subdue your own mind. Do people eat to live, or live to eat? If you live to eat, it is really meaningless. Instead, you should live to do useful things: benefit your family, people, and country. Bring forth the heart of a Bodhisattva."

The Abbot continues at night:

"What is Buddhadharma? Let me ask you, what isn't Buddhadharma? All Dharmas are just the Buddhadharma. Just the everyday common affairs of eating, putting on clothes, sleeping – all this is part of the Buddhadharma. It is a pity that we are immersed every second in Buddhadharma and yet do not recognize it. We go outside seeking for the Dharma.

"The definition of an external way is any seeking outside of one's own mind. If you understand your own mind, see your own nature – this is real Buddhadharma. Do not seek it high and far. Every act, every thought is an enactment of the Buddhadharma. If in every thought you do not create offenses, just this is merit and virtue. However living beings are strange, you tell them to do good and they shirk from it; you don't have to tell them to do evil, they draw near it on their own. Just like children – their parents tell them to be good kids, to follow the rules, and they won't. So it is said,

> Fish jump in the water,
> People mill around the marketplace.
> Not knowing to do good deeds,
> Willingly they create offenses.
> You may pile up gold and silver as high as a mountain,
> But when you close your eyes the last time,
>   all will be gone.
> When you go with empty hands to see King Yama,
> You may finally feel remorse and start to cry.

"King Yama asks you in the hells, 'Why did you commit all these offenses?' and you say, 'But I want to change.' Sorry, too late.

"When Shakyamuni Buddha was on the causal ground, he gave up his body thousands of times for the Dharma. He fed his body to the tiger, to eagles. Once, when cultivating as a patient immortal, he allowed the King of Kalinga to chop off his four limbs without giving rise to a single thought of anger. And now we people should ask ourselves: are we willing to renounce our bodies for the Dharma? Not to talk of an entire body, how about just ten pounds of flesh, or even an ounce? I bet most of us aren't willing to give up even that much."

Heng Sure • August 26, 1978
When Ch'an sitting is good

Time after time on *san bu yi bai*, Heng Ch'au and I realize the central importance of Ch'an meditation. Ch'an sitting is a fragile practice. It is the summit of all other practices – the last Dharma-door attained and the first one lost when one's daily schedule is not rigorously maintained.

It is analogous to tempering a rare metal, or cooking a fine dish. All the preparation must proceed on time, in order, without haste or delay. The ingredients must all be present, the fire must be just hot enough, the cooking time must be precise.

When it's perfect, the process yields pure vajra, the body is transformed, the mind is subdued and still. Afflictions and bad habits are burned away, and the darkness of ignorance yields to wisdom's light.

When Ch'an sitting is good, it changes everything. The daily affairs of life fall into place, the spiritual realm and the mundane world unite, because the mind has stopped discriminating.

When Ch'an sitting is absent, the whole day suffers. Afflictions gather, attachments settle in, bad habits return. Spiritual vision disappears as the deep places of the mind become active again.

There is no mystery to the practice: sitting still for a long time quiets the mind and body profoundly. Not sitting allows the mind to stir and turn like waves on a stormy lake.

Heng Chau • August 26, 1978
The more the better

Hundreds of people come up to bow to the Abbot after these lectures – hundreds upon hundreds so far – all different, all the same.

"Don't keep me waiting, because I vowed not to become a Buddha until all my disciples do," he said to the largest single refuge-taking crowd in the history of Malaysia.

A thousand new disciples, with ten thousand more hassles. Mind boggling! To teach (*hsuan*) and transform (*hua*), the Abbot gives and waits. Each day his load increases. Each day he's happy and untroubled and ready for what comes – "the more the better."

The ocean of the Flower Store World,
Identical with the Dharmarealm, no difference.
Adorned and extremely pure,
They rest peacefully in empty space.

Within the ocean of worlds,
The variety of ksetras are difficult to conceive of.
Each and every one is independent,
One and all they are neither confused nor jumbled.

Avatamsaka Sutra

Desire is the cause of all our troubles and unhappiness. Desire can never be satisfied. The harder you try, the more you hurt, and the further from it you go. I couldn't put down false thoughts about women. It was just ignorance feeding longing. It took near-death to make me realize that desire is really stupid.

Living being's bodies are all different,
They come from adherence
    to the distinctions in thought.
So, too, of the many kinds of ksetras.
None do not come from karma…

According to what living beings practice in their minds,
Their visions of ksetras follow suit.

From the power of living beings' karma
    are produced many lands.

Avatamsaka Sutra

We are all the same, and yet different. What is the same is the true – our Buddhanature, pure, genuine, blissful, and still.

Don't eat meat! We are worried and anxious because we sense our retribution coming from offenses. The anger and resentment stay in the killed animals' flesh, and we eat it. It causes incurable diseases and leaves us looking worried and wrinkled, not clean and bright like children. It makes us old and uptight. Disasters, wars come from acts of killing – eating meat is eating our ancestors and our family. How can this be okay?

August 27, 1978
Day 30 : Alor Setar

The Abbot talks about the need for unity within Buddhism:

"Because I've said a lot of things that people do not like to hear, after I leave, there are bound to be many who will scold me. Now, you who have taken refuge with me should not get upset when this happens. Just bow to these people, and admit that it's your teacher's fault. Don't fight on behalf of your teacher. If I have to rely on my disciples to fight for a good name, I do not deserve to be called your teacher."

Some questions and answers:

Q: "How can we convince people who know only how to bow to the Buddhas to truly investigate the Bodhisattva conduct ?"

A: "Why don't you teach them to be hoodlums instead? Here are people who already know how to bow and recite, which is already much better than doing a lot of other things. Why do you not use your time to convert bad people instead of harping on finer points? In this world, there is no definite standard of good and bad. You say a person is evil, and there are bound to be people more evil than he is; you say a person is good, and there are bound to be people better than he is, too. There are no fixed standards. If people can already recite and bow, isn't this already much better than not reciting at all?"

Q: "If left-home people do not practice the Buddhadharma, can we as laypeople convince them to return to laylife?'"

A: "Better still, why don't you leave home? Just leave home and be a model Sanghan, then you'll show them."

Q: "There are some families in which congenital diseases pass from one generation to the next, is this explainable by cause and effect?"

A: "Of course, heredity is just the same as cause and effect. If there were no causes planted before, there would be no effect. Heredity is just the transmission of the cause from generation to generation. Again, do not nit-pick about details. A person is a person. It's not because his head is on top and his toes below that he's a human being."

The Abbot on compassion:

"Of course, compassion is not mere external show of kindness. The latter falls easily into the realm of artificiality. Compassion arises on its own as you understand more. As you grow up, it flows out from your self-nature because then you are able to really see. The same goes for wisdom. Being able to say the right words at the right time, to be in perfect harmony with the occasion, this is part of genuine wisdom. Now why do people appreciate my way of answering their questions? It's because I don't think. I do not calculate for myself.

"Real eloquence is not something learned or copied from textbooks. It arises spontaneously from your self nature. Whenever you try for an effect, that already is extra baggage, and your speech may end up having an adverse effect. You try to say something striking, and you end up muddling that issue or hurting people's feelings. Don't pretend, don't try to make a good impression. Just be really true; everything else takes care of itself.

"Now, I am one who doesn't think. Even with regard to the City of Ten Thousand Buddhas, I'm not twiddling my thumbs, wondering from where we'll get our next contribution. I just let things happen naturally. Let it flow. I don't think about the past, the present, or the future. My mind is empty.

"People are born alone into this world. Solitary. When I was young and yet a student of the Way, I used to prefer to be by myself. I seldom talked, and I looked really dumb. Many people looked down on me, even novices looked down on me, ordering me to do this and that. And I voluntarily took on menial chores that nobody else wanted to do: washing the vegetables, cooking, cleaning out the pit toilets. I gathered my essence and internal jewels and mixed with the dust. I wasn't about to disclose them to anyone who happened along the way. Even now at Gold Mountain and the City of Ten Thousand Buddhas, I am solitary. I enjoy most being in my little room, doing my own work. Most people who come to talk have nothing of import to say. Why talk for the sake of talking, why waste time on non-essentials?

"When I help people, I don't want it to be known that I am helping them. They need not thank me or become attached to any external aspects of Dharma. Real compassion is often silent."

Heng Sure • August 27, 1978
Bitter lettuce

Abbot: "Don't give me food! Don't serve me! I'm not as greedy as you are!" (then a smile to soften it)

Heng Sure: "That's for certain."

Abbot: "When you see that my bowl is full, why do you pile more on? I can't finish what I've got."

Heng Sure: "My eyes are bigger than my stomach."

Abbot: "Then you should eat with your eyes."

I gave the Abbot a lettuce leaf. "It's really bitter lettuce." He refused it flat. I ate it. Mistake. Right away I felt queasy. Downed some stomach pills after lunch and felt a little better.

Heng Ch'au: "I scan the table and some foods always catch my eye. That lettuce sent my alarms flashing – it absorbed my energy. It was unclean. I didn't tell you because I thought you knew."

Heng Ch'au and I are on parallel tracks again as always. Both of us are recovering our cultivation. We've been down and out since the trip began; now we're pulling it back together with the Abbot's energy guiding us.

Sitting is coming back. The blackouts while bowing are fewer. Eating is slowly coming into control – digestion regular. I can recognize my cultivation head again. Desire is shrinking, after a high flare-up.

Heng Chau • August 27, 1978
Break precepts, there won't be a response

On seeing monks eating meat and smoking in Malaysia.

Major lesson of *san bu yi bai*: what you do is what you get. Karma is not off by a hair. When one person keeps precepts, all living beings benefit – good *chi* in the world increases. When one person breaks precepts, all the world suffers, and the bad *chi* pollutes the air.

Seeing Buddhist disciples who don't keep rules hurts my heart. All that good energy going down the wrong road. Cultivating the Way without strictly holding precepts is like trying to get rice by boiling rocks. No matter how long you cook the rocks, they will never become rice. No matter how long or hard you cultivate (offer incense, bow, recite mantras and sutras, make offerings, take refuge with a hundred Dharma Masters), if you don't keep the precepts, there won't be a response. "The Way and the response intertwine and are hard to conceive of."

Everything that happens to us comes from what we do.
                                        Avatamsaka Sutra

August 28, 1978
Day 31 : Sungei Patani, Kedah

The Abbot on selflessness:

"Never, never be selfish. Don't look out just for your own benefit or put it before everybody else's. The reason for stupidity is selfishness. If you are not selfish, you'll immediately open up great wisdom."

The Abbot about afflictions and vigor:

"When you get to the point of no-seeking, that is no-worrying; the less you know about affairs, the less affliction you have. Otherwise, you'll always be embroiled in the crossfire of the eight sufferings."

"Vigor means not being lazy, not just vigorous for one day and then slack for ten. One has to be vigorous at every moment, day and night, month after month, year after year, lifetime after lifetime. It is easy to bring forth a bold resolve for Bodhi, but it is hard to persist year after year in the same vein. That is the task of a great hero. Like the two monks who are bowing once every three steps. They are not seeking for their own comfort or fame; they've dedicated their lives to all of humanity. This is the path that all Buddhas, Bodhisattvas, and Patriarchs have tread. That is not to say that they are already Buddhas, Bodhisattvas, or Patriarchs, but they are going along the right path. They are two highly intelligent people; they could not have been easily taken in by any clever rap of mine.

"So, we should cultivate the Path with vigor. When you cultivate, do not seek. You shouldn't calculate like this: 'I've just recited the Earth Store Sutra, how much merit have I acquired?' Why don't you ask yourself how many offenses you created before you recited the sutra? Do not keep tabs on the benefit you'll get from reciting the Buddha's name. Cultivation is something you ought to do. It is your duty.

"When people cultivate, they sometimes attain some state or other which they mistake for something fantastic. They think they've obtained spiritual penetrations. Let me tell you, they haven't even attained ghostly penetrations. Don't be deluded like Su Tung P'o (famous fifteenth-century Sung poet, artist, and Ch'an student). One day while sitting in meditation he had a minor state; this inspired him to compose the following verse:

> Bowing to the lord of the skies,
> Your light illumines the thousand universes.
> The eight winds cannot move me,
> Sitting upright upon a purple-gold lotus.

He was extremely pleased with his own verse. Now the eight winds are: praise, ridicule, suffering, joy, benefit, decay, slander, and repute. Su thought he had attained such a high state that he was now in a state of unmoving suchness, even when confronted by the eight winds. He told a messenger to take his verse across the Yangtze River to Dhyana Master Fwo Yin, so that Fwo Yin could certify him. D.M. Fwo Yin took one look at the verse, and without saying a word, wrote four characters on the scroll and sent it back.

"Now, the messenger could not read characters, so he took it right back to Su Tung P'o. Su had expected lofty praises, but when he opened the scroll he had a fit. On it was written in bold strokes, 'Fart! Fart!' He toppled right down from his purple-gold lotus throne!

"He tore over to D.M. Fwo Yin's place and threw a temper tantrum. D.M. Fwo Yin eyed him coolly and said, 'Oh, I thought you were one who is not moved by the eight winds, yet two farts have blown you all the way across the river.' Su Tung P'o knew he'd been had. But it was too late.

"Cultivators should be in control of states; states should not turn people. Cultivators should not get angry, no matter what state they encounter."

About several hundred youngsters shaking the Abbot's hands and calling him with heart-felt warmth:

"These beings were all taught and transformed by me in previous lifetimes, that is why they so spontaneously bring forth their true hearts when they see me again."

Heng Sure • August 28, 1978
Oh well, it's only rice and tofu

It's hard to share this one – a teaching at lunch that took place all in the mind. But it moved events in the outside world all the same.

I ran out of rice. No one was watching me... I thought, "Pull it in. This is good. Your vibes are under control. Take it as it comes. Sit still."

I felt the Abbot monitoring my thoughts. The urge to eat more rice rose again. I looked around – twelve people, all waiting to serve the table, but I was invisible – no one was watching me.

First thought: Irritation! Second thought: "Wait! A good state! Congrat's! You aren't putting out energy or leaking. Wait. Hold on. Maybe this is just how much you should eat. Stop here. No more rice or bread."

I answered myself, "Okay. I'll take a chance and stop here. I feel fine. The reward will pay back in good sitting tonight."

I looked up to see the last plate of tofu being carried away, and my heart dropped for an instant.

"Rats. Okay, that's the signal. Still, a half bowl of rice with some of that tofu would surely be good. Never mind. Be content."

I started into the fruit and subdued the impulse to grab more bread, feeling better and better. The hunger urge was easy to put down, for the first time in a month.

There at my elbow appeared a bowl of rice with a heap of tofu. Wooo! Alarms! No thanks. Test. Heng Ch'au asked for it. Amen, brother. Oops. He only took half. You can't leave half a bowl uneaten. Better finish it. But, you've had enough! Oh well, it's only rice and tofu (famous last words). And down it went. My sincerity was tested and failed. All the laymen were watching closely.

I should have held the line and asked for help. The bowl was not mine in the first place. Heng Ch'au took half, he should have dealt with the rest. My greed ate it down. I felt the Abbot's scanning.

Next thought: some orange juice would be fine; no, I don't need it – I'm over-full now. Forget it. Heng Ch'au turned to me and said, "Want to finish my juice?" Down the hatch. Stuffed belly. False thoughts brought on an unwanted response.

Abbot: "On one hand, all these people think that Americans are marvelous, and on the other they despise you; it's a real contradiction."

Heny Sure: "It's not simple."

Abbot: "On this trip you two are really useful. You have cut through the contradiction to influence a lot of people to cultivate."

Heng Sure: "As long as I don't talk, right?"

Abbot and others in chorus: "Right!" (laughter)

Heng Sure: "As soon as I open my mouth or act or eat, it's all over."

Heng Chau • August 28, 1978
It took nearly dying to wake up

As we sat in a back room of a temple, I vaguely felt my eyes wander about and my energy looking for a place to play or latch onto. Suddenly I felt compelled to look at the Abbot. He was staring right through me – eyes big and focused, face indescribable and without expression – I couldn't look at him and averted my eyes. But it put me on ice. The Abbot was just helping me out with a glance… levels within levels, worlds within worlds. The Abbot teaches deeply and silently.

Heng Sure and I are entering into deeper levels only as we bow and sit long and hard. The Abbot is there at every turn with guidance and patient support. We fumble, lose faith, go off and play, retreat to worldly dharmas, seek outside. But we keep coming back to the Ultimate. And the Abbot waits and laughs, "With me, everything's okay."

To move from one level of cultivation to the next takes all the strength and skill one can muster. It's so easy to go backward – no limit ahead. Faith, faith, and patience. "Hard work and patience." New towns and lands – same rules and one map.

Basically I got turned. The intensity and pitch kept accelerating, and I lost control. The transit room in Manila was the turning point. On the outside I held tight, but my thoughts were false and running like a mountain-spring creek – the old *mau bing* = ego + women. I couldn't stop it even when I wanted to. Malacca was the climax, and I went down hard. It's a long way from King Yama to the Pure Land – a long, single thought.

This Malacca Massacre was just the extreme of the cause and effect of false thinking experienced on *san bu yi bai*. I'm slow and hard to change in some ways. It took nearly dying to wake me up a little. Stupid! The Abbot's instructions and lectures in Los Angeles all contain the warnings and solutions, but I didn't take them seriously – casual and sloppy. Thinking it was still okay to false think – thinking that *san bu yi bai's* large purpose would wait while I dilly-dallied around in my petty ego trips.

"When you're out of money, go back to work." I feel different.

August 29, 1978
Day 32 : Khota Bharu, Kelantan

The Abbot in his arrival speech at the Kelantan Buddhist Association,

"In studying the Buddhadharma, don't seek high and wide, but seek it right within the common affairs of your daily life. To get to the far, you have to start from the near, to get to the high, you have to start from the low. It means within every thought, word, and deed, returning the light and shine within."

At night, the Abbot to an audience of seven hundred:

When cultivating, be careful about cause and effect. Do not be the least bit casual about what you say, don't recklessly slander people, and don't use a common person's measure to estimate a sage. I'll relate an account of something that happened in Hong Kong, though many people probably will not want to believe it. There was an elderly laywoman in her sixties named Liu Kuo Chuen who took refuge with me. She started eating pure food, and whenever I lectured the sutras she would not miss one session, otherwise she'd feel very uncomfortable. But the strange thing was that she was deaf: she couldn't hear a word. At that time, I was at Hsi Le Yuan, (Western Bliss Gardens) which was built on a mountainside, and to get up to the monastery one had to climb up a steep flight of three hundred stairs. It was hard for her, but she always came.

One day during a sutra lecture she suddenly heard the phrase, "Homage to the Lotus Pool Assembly of Buddhas and Bodhisattvas," and thereupon promptly opened up her hearing. She was no longer deaf! From then on, she cultivated even more ardently. However,

If you want to become a Buddha,
You may run into demons;
If you want to be good,
Your karmic obstacles catch up with you.

There was something she had refused to believe in her past life and in this life she had to undergo a retribution for that disbelief. Several hungry ghosts came to dwell in her stomach. One night, she dreamt that three fat children entered her stomach, and from that day on, she had to eat about eight meals a day. She had to eat a full meal every hour.

This perturbed her to no end. She consulted both Chinese and Western doctors, and none of them could discover the source of her illness. After about a year of this wearisome malady, one day she said to me,

"Shih Fu, there is someone in my stomach who talked to me."

I asked her, "What did it say?"

"Well, this morning I was making oil cakes, when this voice from my stomach started whining, 'No, I don't like oil cakes!'"

And what did you tell it?

"I said, 'It doesn't matter whether you like it or not, I just have to fill you up.'"

I answered, "Even if there was a baby inside your stomach, it still wouldn't talk. There must be something weird in there. Tonight before you go to sleep, light a stick of incense and bow before the Buddha; then observe what happens."

That night, she lit a stick of incense and bowed, and, just as she was about to doze off, she saw Wei To Bodhisattva come with a bowl of noodles in his hand. He put the bowl down and the three chubby children scrambled out of Liu Kuo Chuen's stomach, gulping down the noodles as fast as they could. Wei To Bodhisattva grabbed each one of them by the ear and spirited them away. From that moment on she felt her stomach had become empty. She no longer had to wolf down eight meals a day.

So, ultimately, who were those three kids? They were three monsters: two huge lizards and a big frog. And why did she contract such an illness? It was because in her previous life she encountered someone with exactly the same illness. A Dharma Master who healed that person told her about the two lizards and the frog, and she wouldn't believe it. "Now that's what I call a bunch of superstitious rot!" she said. And because she had said something wrong in disbelief, this lifetime she got to experience the illness first hand. So from this incident, you should know the intensity of erring in cause and effect.

It is said that Bodhisattvas fear causes but do not fear the effect, whereas common people fear effects but do not fear causes. The Bodhisattva is extremely careful on the causal ground not to make mistakes so that on the effect ground he is no longer afraid – he figures he's only reaping what he deserves. Living beings, however, are just the opposite. They do not fear the causes they plant. They recklessly go about killing, stealing, lying, indulging in deviant sex, and taking intoxicants, yet when the retribution catches up with them, they are scared out of their wits. It's said that if you kill someone's father, somebody else will kill your own father. Cause and effect work unerringly. If you plant good causes, you will reap good effects; if you plant evil causes, you will reap evil effects. If you plant tomatoes, you won't get red peppers. If you're filial to your parents now, later on your children will be filial to you. There is a saying that,

> Families that do good
>   always enjoy good fortune;
> Families that do evil are plagued
>   with early deaths and many disasters.
> The rewards for good and retributions for evil
>   follow us like a shadow.

Everything that befalls you, whether good or bad, comes not of itself but as a direct response to your actions. Effects are never off by a hair's breadth.

We should not be confused about cause and effect. When Dhyana Master Pai Chang was lecturing the sutras, an old man with a white beard used to come to listen. One night, the old man stayed behind. D.M. Pai Chang asked him who he was, and it turned out that he was an old fox who lived in the mountains beyond.

"Prior to this, I was a left-home person," he explained. "Once, someone asked me, 'Do great cultivators fall under the rule of cause and effect?' At that time I replied, 'Great cultivators do not come under the rule of cause and effect.' Here I made a great mistake. Even the Bodhisattvas fear causes and do not fear effects, how much the more should great cultivators be wary of cause and effect. Because I answered incorrectly, I received the retribution of a fox's body for the next five hundred lives. Now, can the venerable master help me?"

D.M. Pai Chang told him, "You can ask me the same question now."

The old man asked, "Do great cultivators come under the rule of cause and effect?"

D.M. Pai Chang answered, "Great cultivators are not confused by cause and effect."

It's the word "not confused" that's the key. Cultivators are very clear about cause and effect; they have to thoroughly understand its workings. Upon hearing this, the old man became enlightened. He took leave of D.M. Pai Chang, saying, "Now I can go off to rebirth, you can find me in the mountains yonder."

The next day, D.M. Pai Chang went looking for the fox's whereabouts, and sure enough, in the cave he'd been directed to lay a fox's corpse. D.M. Pai Chang cremated it with a ceremony befitting a Sanghan.

Some questions and answers:

Q: "Is there a God or not; how would you describe him?"

A: "If you say there is a God, then there is one; if you say there isn't any God, then there isn't any. Why? Because if in your mind there is a God, then he exists; if in your mind there is no God, then he doesn't exist. You look all around you and you can't see God, you can't pin him down. Yet, many people believe in him because of faith. All dharmas are created from the mind alone."

Q: (For Prof. Kuo K'ung) "When you say that Buddhism is science and science is just Buddhism, what do you mean?"

A: "When I say that Buddhism is science and science is just Buddhism, I enlarge both domains. Buddhism is the study of the truth of the mind – if expanded it also covers the study of all material bodies. Science is the study of the truth of material bodies – if enlarged its scope includes the study of the mind as well. Now, the Abbot says that science is included within Buddhism, something which most people find harder to understand. 'Everything is made from the mind alone,' so if you investigate things to the ultimate, there are really no material bodies, no science – there isn't even a thing! Everything is empty, but from this emptiness arises existence. Now, in physics we can break down matter into more and more infinitesimal particles – from the atom, to the neutron, to the newly-discovered J-particle. You can say that this particle exists in a 'field.' A 'field' is so wonderful because it defies normal description. If you say that it exists, then there is not a thing, if you say it does not exist, all things come from it."

The arrival of the delegates at the Kelant

...ddhist Association, Khota Bharu

Heng Chau • August 29, 1978
Rice water fields and jungles

Leave Penang for Kota Baru.

Breakfast at D.M. Chu Mor's. Airport send-off.

Heng Sure: "It's like Brigadoon. Nothing's what it seems."

Yeah! In Manila I scattered by watching stewardesses, and became blind and confused. This time I didn't run outside chasing the six dusts and "saw" things a little more clearly. The airport was full of danger – bad energy and hexes carried by or concentrated in people – subtle, too quick to think about – have to go on with the "reading" before the first impression fades like assassins in masquerade waiting and watching for an opening in the group – any crack will do. Whatever our weak point – *mau bing* – that's where they hit.

I watch the Abbot for the cues – "roll it up, let it go" – eye glances, nudges, a question, "go check this out." Under it all it's learning to be mind-ground warriors, but nobody knows, nobody sees, and who would believe?

Rice water fields, jungle, the red ground, and tile roof-tops blend and fade as we take off for the East Coast, and what next?

In flight the work goes on. The Abbot saves Kuo Kuei from a sticky stewardess. Tuning, adjusting, relaxing, and tightening – the Abbot guards and teaches each of us. What a school! The Dharmarealm and the self-nature, like clouds in the sky – now separate, now the same – always changing and interchanging, never the same, no place to rely on.

> …the Dharmarealm and the self-nature are not two.
>
> Avatamsaka Sutra

At the risk of seeming simplistic, there's something going on between the forces of good and evil. We see it all the time, and as our cultivation deepens, so does this awareness. True, all this good and bad energy begins in a single thought, but the manifestations and proportions it takes are really mind-blowing. Variations of greed, hatred, and ignorance swelling and uniting to the size of a world war or collision of galaxies, or shrinking down to the size of the *gu* poison and a gecko lizard.

Landing in Kota Baru, the land is a sheet of muddy water; the sky and clouds are reflected in it, making the earth look like a mirage, a transparent sheet of film. So it is.

All activities are impermanent,
Characterized by production and extinction.
When production and extinction are ended,
That still extinction is bliss.

People love the Abbot. They love to see him, hear him, get scolded by him, laugh with him. He is the rare one within the rare, a living tradition that all have given up for dead. His deportment and wit, his kindness and thought-free wisdom disarms and gathers in even the most skeptical and stiff.

In cultivating, there's no big or small. The big is just a dimension of the small. The small is the parent of the big. On one hand, the measure of our minds is stretched and expanded to the limits of empty space. On the other, the mind dangles on a single bit of food. In a very real way, the tiny and the vast interfuse and are not two. When the mind is clear and pure about food and clothes and sleep, for example, then all the tubes and doors stay open, and the Avatamsaka world is everywhere and unobstructed. When the mind is turned and confused by food, sex, or sleep, the world is jumbled and fragmented, and every move is like jamming a broom handle through the spokes of a moving bicycle tire.

August 30, 1978
Day 33 : All is number one, there is no number two

The Abbot in an evening address:

"In cultivating, you have to do it reliably, honestly, down-to-earth. It means not being lazy, it means following the rules. Don't go seeking for a side door, a short cut to cultivation. All you need to do is to enter deeply into whatever Dharma-door you choose. You shouldn't be standing on top of one mountain and peering across to another, thinking the grass is greener on the other side. So you recite the Buddha's name for three days, practice the teaching school for three days, and sit in Ch'an for three days – if you are just hopping back and forth, you'll have no accomplishment. Why? Because you haven't been reliable; you haven't focused on one Dharma-door. It is said,

> In single-mindedness there is efficacy,
> In diversity you just become scattered.

"Of the eighty-four thousand Dharma-doors, all are number one; there is no number two. Whatever is most opportune for you is number one. So don't be greedy, don't bite off more than you can chew for you may not even digest the material. If you vacillate back and forth, first dabbling in the Apparent School, then the Secret School, and then reciting the Buddha's name, and so on, always working on superficial aspects, you are not being reliable.

"In cultivation, the most important thing is not to give rise to doubt. If you don't doubt, but maintain deep faith, you'll bring forth great wisdom. Having wisdom just means no longer being confused and upside-down.

"'Prajna' is a Sanskrit word which means wisdom, but because it also carries other connotations, it's treated as an honorific and not translated. There are three types of Prajna:

1. Literary Prajna – the sutras and all words which can lead you to wisdom.

2. Contemplative and Illuminating Prajna – use your wonderful contemplative wisdom and illumine all dharmas. Deeply enter the Sutra Store and obtain wisdom like the sea.

3. True Mark Prajna – The true mark is just no mark, the real appearance of all dharmas is emptiness."

The Abbot then comments on Ch'an…

"'Dhyana' is a Sanskrit word which means 'cultivation of the mental process,' (思惟修) and 'quiet ponderance' (靜慮). It means thinking, but investigating a *hua t'ou* (話頭), examining the meditation topic before it has formed into a thought. You ask, 'Who is mindful of the Buddha?' Who is mindful? 'Well of course it's me,' you say. Who are you? Are you your body? What happens to you after this body dies? After the body is cremated, where do you go? Behind this stinking skin-bag, who is the real you?

"You investigate this topic back and forth, in every single thought – you force it to a head:

> When the mountains are exhausted
>   and the waters dried up,
> And you think there is no way out,
> Suddenly, amidst the dark willows and bright flowers
> Is another village…

Break through! In investigating Ch'an, you are just getting rid of the false. For each fraction of the false you rip off, there appears an equivalent fraction of truth.

"In investigating Ch'an, after your skill is developed you may enter progressively into the heavens of the four dhyanas. But, do not think that you can certify yourself in any of these states. Only a Good Knowing Advisor is able to certify your level of accomplishment. And even then it's not a big deal. You haven't certified to any fruit even upon reaching the fourth dhyana. The four dhyanas are just the beginning stages of cultivation.

"The worst pitfall in Ch'an is engaging in Ch'an banter, or head-mouth Zen. People who rave on about Ch'an usually do not know a thing about it. In 1968 such a 'head-mouth patriarch' came to see me at Buddhist Lecture Hall. He said that he'd been certified by the Buddhist association of some country and has advertised in some papers that he is enlightened. I said, 'You have no shame; what type of enlightenment have you opened?'

"He answered, 'The enlightenment of the Sixth Patriarch, which is the same as the enlightenment of Shakyamuni Buddha.'

"'In that case I can chop off your head right now. After the Sixth Patriarch entered into the stillness, a Korean wanted to chop off his head and bring it back to Korea to make offerings to it. Since you're enlightened I can do it to you while you're still alive.'

"That did it; he was scared out of his wits and never dared come back!"

Heng Sure • August 30, 1978
Like bees to honey

Lessons in worldly wisdom. The closest people to us are enemies of Buddhism. Spies, informers, goblins, and agents, laws, and fear and loathing.

The Abbot: "This is life and death. That we haven't lost anyone is doing pretty good – you might say it's been perfect so far. So be careful from here on out.

"This trip has been a groundbreaker. To have so many people attend, like bees to honey, is unprecedented. You couldn't force so many people to crowd together in the way they do. It's because we are unmoved by conditions. I have much more that I want to say, but the potentials for hearing it must be there. I always accord with opportunities in speaking the Dharma."

Heng Chau • August 30, 1978
It will not snow

Sick again; cause unknown. The Abbot kept asking me who I talked to after the evening lecture (Kuo T'ung lied to me so he could stay and watch a film.) I felt two zaps during the film – the second one started the whole room spinning, and I felt as if I was floating away. I recited twenty-seven lines of the Shurangama Mantra and things returned to "normal," more or less.

I spent the afternoon and evening sitting in Ch'an, reciting the Great Compassion Mantra, and sleeping. Weak, cold symptoms, loss of fluids, headache, fatigue.

Was it anger, a hex, or a leak? Things are either getting more subtle, or I'm getting more confused. Cause and effect isn't clear as when we are bowing up the coast of California. For a month I've felt strong and healthy for no more than five or six days. I really don't care about the suffering; it is not knowing the causes that is hard to take. I feel like I'm fighting against an invisible opponent for my life.

The Abbot told Kuo Lei to come with the group to Singapore – he'll guarantee no snow in Nepal until Kuo Lei gets down from the mountains. "What can I say?" asked Kuo Lei.

Terengganu Buddhist Association
August, 1978

August 31, 1978
Day 34 : Terengganu

The Abbot on Dharma doors:

"No matter what Dharma-door you cultivate, just do it reliably and honestly. Don't flirt with different doors, opting for the sensational and bizarre. Actual cultivation is very modest; it is plain living from day to day. If you're not too big for the commonplace, you won't be too small when something special happens. How often do we set our gaze upon the heavens with our legs planted in mud. How often do we seek outside of ourselves for Dharma, looking far and high for something which is right underneath our very noses!"

Heng Chau • August 31, 1978
You don't have to talk to women at all

Message:

"Patience. Things will work themselves out naturally."
The Abbot

My body grows weaker, but my resolve is even stronger. This constant malaise brings a certain clear view to things and their impermanence. The dead-bird approach for pulling back the light through the six roots is the key, but not easy to sustain.

The Abbot again stressed not talking with women, "As a novice you don't have to talk with women at all."

My appetite for the world and women has shrunk since Malacca and now again with this present illness. The nature of the man-woman desire thing is becoming clearer; that is, clearer on a gut level, not just on the surface (head). Ignorance has to be ended in the first five consciousnesses, as well as in the sixth. What we normally call "understanding" is past words and thought and reached only by cultivation and the help of a good and wise teacher.

September 1, 1978
Day 35 : From being angry to being stupid

The Abbot speaks against superstition and the custom of burning paper money:

"People ask me whether there are ghosts or not. If in your mind there are ghosts, it's a case of people being afraid of ghosts; if in your mind there are no ghosts, then ghosts are afraid of people. Because of greed, people do all sorts of upside-down things that they know are irrational, like burning paper money with the Rebirth Mantra on it. This offense – that of destroying the Buddha's image and burning the sutras – is grave enough to send you into the relentless hells. Some people are smarter still – even before they die, they start depositing money into the banks of the shadowy regions. These people already know where they're heading. They think they can bribe King Yama. How pitiful!

"People are turned forever by the three poisons. We end up as people again because we're addicted to this poisonous wine. Just think, as soon as a baby is born, he is already greedy. He is greedy for his mother's milk. Who teaches him to be greedy? Nobody. This is just a hangover from timeless kalpas. And, when the baby is not greedy for milk, he is greedy for sleep. Even if he is satiated, he is not really happy. The first sound which an infant utters upon leaving his mother's womb is 'Ku! Ku! Ku!' (the word in Chinese means both 'to cry' and 'to suffer') – he knows it is a lot of suffering to be here.

"As the child grows older, it becomes greedier still for new clothes and toys. What child isn't greedy for new toys? You deprive him of something and he throws a fit. This anger results from unful-filled desire. And as he develops, he'll do even more absurd things when his needs are not fulfilled. He goes from being angry to being stupid. We are all helplessly manipulated by greed, anger, and stupidity. Wouldn't you say this is pathetic?"

Heng Sure • September 1, 1978
Tell them to go right, they go left

Outer-space time. I caught a cold in the Mercedes yesterday morning. Inevitable. It hit me like a monsoon. Drip. *Tai chi chuan* brought me back – one hour later, the big dive again. *Yang-yin* flip-flop.

The group is at a low ebb this week. Cracks are showing, patience is short. The Abbot at the center is unmoving and twinkling.

Being a Shih Fu must be an awesome hassle – what a grind. Tell them to go right and they go left. Tell them it's going to hurt, and they grab it even harder. When the evil darkness is strong, the good light must be nurtured and cared for. Let the darkness go, and the light grows all by itself.

Kuo Lei left the group in Terengganu. It feels like a mistake in judgment. He wants to beat the snow in the Himalayas – plans to be there for three months, but couldn't stay with his teacher for two more weeks, even when asked to stay. The Abbot so rarely requests anything of anyone – it must be important to keep the group together. But Kuo Lei's fierce independence (or selfish attachments) blinded him to this path. Too bad. I'm disappointed.

Heng Chau • September 1, 1978
If a person can sit still for a moment

All the talk stopped this afternoon as thirty or so people in Terengganu gathered to recite Earth Store Bodhisattva's name and then sat silently. That's what I'd like to see more of, because that's where it's at.

"If a person can sit still for a moment, it is worth more than building as many pagodas of the gems as there are grains of sand in the Ganges."

And certainly worth ten thousand times that number of words.

Ch'an.

To be able to teach and transform without making a mess requires unwavering Ch'an concentration. To be able to save and take across without getting turned by states takes a lot of samadhi power.

San bu yi bai was quickly developing into a non-ending session of silence, reduction of food, clothes, and sleep, long bowing, and long sitting. The basics. Progress is slow but real. One word too many, an extra bite of food, a stray, unchecked false thought brought its retribution immediately ("instant karma").

In Los Angeles, or bowing through the cities, our samadhi power and dharma vessels got tested. Almost always, we got turned by good food, fame, women, offerings, and talking too much. But slowly, even here, we started to recognize and change and learn. Malaysia for me was a massive defeat. But I learned a lot too. Mostly my resolve for the Way has deepened and matured. The dead-end emptiness of all worldly dharmas and my ego ignorance appears clearer than ever before.

I feel as though a chunk of fat and a cesspool of old poison is being purged. My body suffers, but my heart is true and my mind solid. In the end, I keep coming back to the wordless interchange between myself and the Abbot in the kitchen of Gold Mountain at the end of the Great Compassion Mantra session.

"There's so much to cut through. How can I ever manage to go back out and do what needs to be done and not get lost or despair?"

"Hard work and patience."

From the beginning to the end it's all just a mess of states and tests. And hard work and patience overcomes all.

A cobra snake shows up during *t'ai chi* – crawled out of durian fruit. Some kids scoop it up and dump it in the high grass across the road. Mosquitoes are heavy here. We're in humid jungle. Tomorrow we go four to five hours south into virgin jungle.

"Bowing almost always makes me happy."

The laymen are starting to look brighter outside and quieter inside. Their speeches ring truer and come from the heart.

Dream.

I'm trying to elude a heavy demonic force following me. I take refuge in a lodge somewhere in a broad and wooded forest. As I warm myself by a fireplace, the demon arrives by carriage and charges in through the front door. It's a woman, her face covered by hair. She's powerful and unafraid. We struggle. I bite her finger – no effect, like soft rubber. Then I bite her whole hand – the same. She laughs sarcastically. The five-line mantra from the Shurangama Mantra comes to my lips over and over, and then I wake up.

It's so real! I feel her waiting for me to fall asleep and go at it again. I do the forty-second and recite the Great Compassion Mantra. Suddenly these words come to mind: "Don't try to beat her; just don't move!" This rings true, and I return to sleep feeling strengthened by these words. No more hassles. The Abbot spoke the words.

September 2, 1978
Day 36 : Pahang Buddhist Association – Kuantan

After a big lunch, the Abbot speaks to the crowd briefly,

"Buddhism is not something esoteric or far-out; rather, it is just the common part of everyday living. Worldly living and Buddhism should be integrated. We should not be turned by states. When something pleasant comes your way, do you become happy? When something unpleasant comes your way, are you disturbed? That's just being turned by states. When unpleasant situations come we should take them in stride. That's what cultivation is about."

The Abbot talks about the vows of Universal Worthy Bodhisattva:

"Don't think that the Buddhas of the future are very far off – it may just mean you, me, and them. All living beings can eventually become Buddhas. Now, in most other religions, bowing and prostrating yourself is considered something below people's standards; they call it 'worshipping idols.' However, in Buddhism, the purpose of bowing is to get rid of our arrogance. When you bow, you put down the pridefulness in yourself and pay homage to the Buddhas of the three periods of time and the ten directions. Bowing is also a great form of exercise! Your body, blood, and breath get a good workout. You won't be bothered by rheumatism or arthritis any more."

The Abbot goes on to discuss the merits of reciting:

"'Namo Amito Fo.' 'Homage to Amita Buddha.' If we return our lives in respect to Amitabha and recite his name constantly with one mind, at death we will not be confused or scattered; we will quickly be reborn in the Land of Ultimate Bliss.

"Why? Because Amitabha, on the causal ground, was a bhikshu who made forty-eight vows. He was determined to cross living beings over from this world of suffering to the world of pure joy. In the Land of Ultimate Bliss, people are not born of parents but from lotuses. There are nine grades of lotuses, and each grade has within it another nine divisions, so altogether there are eighty-one grades. The more one recites, the larger one's lotus becomes and the larger the Buddha sitting upon it."

Heng Sure • September 2, 1978
It fills you full of desire

This limbo is getting to me. My patience is on the brink. My wisdom life is covered by a sticky film of selfishness, like a surgeon's glove. It's too close to the eye to see – I can't grab it because it covers the hand that would grab.

Everything I want to do is waiting for me to break through. Everyone I work with is watching me struggle and spin in the same circles.

Like a timid swimmer, pacing on the cliff forever – not daring to jump in, not willing to stay on the shore, fighting with doubt and fearing failure.

Kuo T'ung told the story of the exploding 7-Up bottle and the Abbot's warning of two weeks ago:

"Any more 7-Up and the bottle will break."

I said, "When he drinks sugar he gets all…"

"*Hun*!" (dizzy) said the Abbot.

"And it's just as if he were drunk," I added.

"Oh, so you can't drink sweet things?" asked Ng Fung Pao.

"Cultivators who drink sugar lose all their samadhi. It scatters. I don't dare eat or drink sugar."

"It fills you full of desire," said the Master.

"Exactly! Right on!" I chimed in.

"So you see?" said the Abbot, "Off by just a hair in the beginning, off by a thousand miles in the end. If you're lacking just that little bit, then you won't be able to collect your concentration when you want to."

The delegation performs prayers

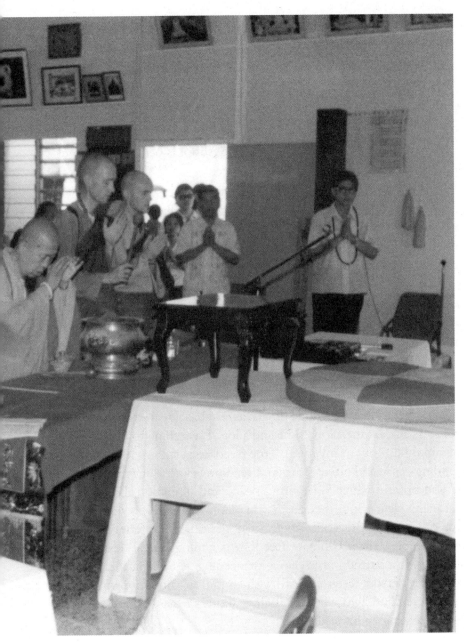
at a small temple in Kuantan, Pahang

Heng Chau • September 2, 1978
Not just storybook tales

Hot, muggy, three and a half hour drive down the eastern coast. A South Pacific-type scene – thatched houses on stilts, people in wrap-around skirts and no tops, tall palm trees, and the ocean.

There are vibes of Malacca here. The Abbot is being very careful about food and drink.

We rely on the Abbot more than we realize and less than we should. That is, the Abbot protects and cues us all often without our knowing it. And as Americans, we insist on strutting out on our own and being independent when we are obviously in a position that requires constant guidance and submission to rules.

I almost blew it by casually letting the Abbot's thermos and some herbs float loosely around. We all know now that hexes and spells and strange poisons are not just storybook tales. They are all too real, especially in this part of the world. We are naive and unexposed but learning fast.

Freedom.

Kuo Lei took off for the Himalayas. He has a real strong urge for freedom. It took me a long time and a lot of searching to finally leave the mountains out of my mind. True freedom is within. It's in understanding cause and effect (karma). Freedom is knowing which things tie you up and which ones bring peace and liberation. Freedom is just being clear about the causes you plant. Liberation is the fruit of true causes. The precepts, strictly held, get rid of the fetters of your own independence. Ultimate freedom is ending sexual desire. Not longing for a partner, not seeking or needing, is to be sufficient and your own person, free to accord with conditions and opportunities – unhindered and light, yet always clear about karma – and so careful, "as if crossing an icy stream."

Not relying on others, taking things as they come – the Universe is your body, all beings are your family. Simple and uncovered, as if living alone in the high mountains.

This is the biggest lesson of *san bu yi bai*: like cause, like result. Wherever you are, you are never outside of your karmic net. To the extreme we have learned to be careful about causes. When the mind is forgotten (concentrated without ever a thought of concentration), then all your steps naturally accord with the Way.

> As the causes, so the results;
> Look within.
> With reverence coming and going,
> Impartial is the Way.

September 3, 1978
Day 37 : Living beings need patience

At night the Abbot gives a moving address:

"It's said that if your offenses weren't heavy, you wouldn't have been born in the Saha, if your karma isn't empty, you won't be born in the Pure Land. In one enlightened thought, one is the Buddha; in one confused thought, one is a living being. The only difference between a Buddha and a common person is that one has great wisdom and one has great stupidity. The reason why our wisdom-light is obstructed is because of our sense of self. We are so attached to this self, always claiming 'I, me, mine', yet at the time of death we'll still have to put it down.

"Since you're so attached to this 'self,' let's investigate and try to locate it now. In your entire body, every single part has its own name – a head is called a head, a hand a hand, a toe a toe – in fact, even the tiniest cell has its own name. Where can you find this thing called the 'self'? Because of this 'self,' you're afraid of getting cold, becoming hungry, and all sorts of other things. There is a clever old saying that goes:

> To reach seventy is already rare;
> Then take off the years of youth and old age;
> What is left in between is not much,
> And even then, half of it is spent on sleep.

It's already rare to get to be seventy years of age; when you take off fifteen years for youth and fifteen years for old age, you end up with about forty years. Half of that is spent in sleeping. Of the remaining twenty years, what about all the time you spend in eating, drinking, putting on clothes, going to the toilet, socializing, coming and going, etc.? – at least another five years down the drain. What do you do with the remaining fifteen years? Most people bungle their way through and don't even know that time is passing. So we go through our lives all muddled. Everything is unreal – all is an illusion. What is so important to attach to? If you see through all and put it down, you'll obtain self-mastery. If you do not put it down, you'll never be truly at ease.

"Many of us create offenses because of this 'self.' Some people within Buddhism even claim that when one dies it's like an 'extinguished lamp,' that there is nothing more after death. If it's truly like this, why bother to study Buddhism at all? You can go ahead and kill and rob or do anything you please. Why are people exhorted to do good and to avoid evil? Just because there is cause and effect.

"Can a person mold his or her own destiny? Yes.

> A superior person realizes
>   that he is creating his own destiny.
> Our fate is determined by us;
>   we seek our own blessings.
> Disasters and blessings have no door;
>   we ourselves search for ways to enter into them.
> The rewards for doing good and the retributions
>   for doing evil follow us like a shadow.

"Most common people are restrained by their fate. An uncommon person is not. If you are an unusually good person, then the good you do transcends the normal boundaries of fate; the same applies if you are an extremely evil person. There is nothing fixed about fate. It is flexible – you can change it from bad to good. Or, if your fate was originally good and you deliberately do a lot of evil, then your good fate will sour too. Therefore, be very careful in whatever you do; do not deliberately go down the wrong track when you know you shouldn't do it all along.

"Many Chinese believe in *feng shui* (geomancy; literally, 'wind and water'). They consult a geomancer to see if they can hit it rich or become an official or have a long life. People who are superstitious say that the wind and water is in direct relation to the geomantic lay-out of the land; they do not know that it's ultimately controlled by a tiny square-inch within your mind. If you have Way-virtue, if you practice meritorious deeds, even a piece of land with poor *feng shui* will become good. Conversely, if you have no Way-virtue, even if you are offered prize wind and water, it will still turn rotten.

"'Merit is the basis, wealth is just a branch.' Do not vie for fame and gain; rather, vie to do good deeds. This means benefiting others – not just one or two individuals – but being selfless and bringing forth a Bodhisattva resolve to help all living beings.

When the Way is lofty,
> dragons and tigers are subdued.
When virtue is abundant,
> ghosts and spirits respect you.

"Most living beings never admit to their own mistakes; they'd rather blame the heavens or other people but not themselves. Daily they become more confused. Those who study Buddhism should not start blaming the Buddhas, saying, 'I've studied Buddhism for three years now; how come I still haven't opened up wisdom?' as if the Buddhas were unfair. Thinking in this way, you create all sorts of karma that is a mixture of good and bad. Instead, you should ask yourself, 'Have I truly gotten rid of my greed, anger, and stupidity?'

"Someone else asks, 'I've been eating vegetarian food; how come my lot has not improved?' or, 'I've been bowing to the Buddhas till calluses have appeared on my head, so how come the Buddhas still don't aid me?' This is called blaming the heavens and finding fault with the Way. For example, I've been transmitting two of the Forty-two Hands and Eyes. Someone who had been cultivating it for three days came and asked me, 'How is it that I still do not have eyes in my hands?' If this were so easy, it would be more popular than smoking opium. Living beings need patience.

"Now, the two monks bowing once every three steps have some of that patience. They've been bowing since May 7, 1977 – sixteen months now. It might take them a total of two and a half years to complete their journey. They're never lazy, not even for a second. The highway in California is extremely hot, and often their hands, feet, and heads hurt so badly it's as if they are being cut with daggers. Yet, they endure it and persevere. This has moved the dragons and gods of the eightfold division, and a series of remarkable responses has occurred.

"In the Sutra of the Forty-two Sections the Buddha said that to make offerings to a thousand evil people is not worth the merit of making an offering to one good person; making offerings to a thousand good people does not equal the merit of making an offering to one person who keeps the five precepts; making offerings to ten thousand such people is not worth making offerings to one bhikshu; making offerings to a hundred thousand bhikshus is not worth making offerings to a First Fruit Arhat; and so on and so forth, to the point that if you were to make offerings to boundless sages, the merit would not measure up to making offerings to a person who has no mark of cultivation or certification, a person of the Way with no mind.

"You can say that these two monks are cultivators of the Way with no mind. They don't strike up many false thoughts each day. In bringing them to Malaysia, you people are reaping measureless merit and virtue by making offerings to them. Now, it is not that I particularly favor the people in Malaysia, rather it is because we've built up Dharma conditions for a very long time. Otherwise, you couldn't bring forth such faith in me over a brief period of time like this. Whatever I say, you people really like to hear; even if I am scolding you, you still eat it up. That's just because we've known each other for countless lifetimes. If you don't believe me, perhaps your dreams will convince you."

Somebody says, "Well, a dream isn't real."

"I didn't tell you it was real, did I? What is real anyway, tell me?"

Ng Fung Pao says, "Cultivating is real."

The Abbot retorts, "Then why don't you cultivate?" (all-round laughter) He continues:

"If in this world you're trying to find the real, you won't be able to. Cultivation is true, but it is not something you can see, per se. The cultivation that you see is already bound to form and shape. If you want to seek the real, first search within the false. Do not seek the real apart from the false. And be patient.

"I'll tell you another story about Kuo Chen (Heng Sure – 'fruit of the truth' and 'constantly real' respectively). The first time we went to take a look at the City of Ten Thousand Buddhas he exclaimed, 'This place is truly good!' At the time I asked him, 'What is "truly good"? If you were to seek all over the world, you'd probably not find anything truly good.' Right then I helped him plant the seed for bowing once every three steps. Just one sentence – yet it inspired him. He became determined to find out what is 'truly good' within himself."

Questions and answers:

Q: "How do you find the real within the false?"

A: "Real diamonds and gold can be obtained from the earth."

Q: "Can we use our minds to understand the three periods of time – the past, present, and future?"

A: "Of course, the three periods of time are just yesterday, today, and tomorrow – what's so hard to fathom? If I explain them as a shorter period of time like this, it will be easier for you to remember and comprehend. The same applies to last year, this year, and next year; this life, last life, and next life. It's all the same theory. If you cannot even remember all that you did yesterday, not to speak of last year, how much the less will you remember your previous lives?"

Heng Chau • September 3, 1978
Exactly what I didn't want to do

"Bowing is just to get your insides to obey you."

Cultivation is to return your light and take charge of yourself, instead of following your six roots and being led around by the nose. Ch'an is the ultimate expression and practice of this *gung fu*; it's for those who want to stand on their own two feet and become a Buddha by their own efforts in this very life.

The Abbot on travelling to a foreign land.

"Stretch your vision to cover all the possibilities and variables. Don't wait until it's too late."

The Abbot has mastered the square inch, so in the smallest gestures he sees their interpenetration with the large: "Everything is made from the mind alone." Activity reveals the mind; the mind directs action.

"Be really careful when leaving – lots of things can happen right at the last few minutes before departing," warned the Abbot.

The Abbot asked me to speak Dharma – exactly what I didn't want to do: talk publicly. He had me talk the previous night also. My emperor sickness (arrogance), almost always comes out when I open my mouth. If I had really seen through the emptiness of self, then there would be no problem speaking in front of a large audience. But, I am intimidated by a large group, and my trying to avoid talking is an attempt to avoid facing my faults, which is an attempt to maintain the fake self. Fear and seeking are just different sides of egoism.

This is really the heart of it: my ego is so strong that I try to cover it rather than face it and toss it out. Whatever I fear or whatever I seek out is just a cue that the self is involved. Seeking seclusion and the fear of public speaking are both trying to cover up the garbage with the rug.

How easy it is to attach to a state (seclusion) or a dharma (silence) and think you're cultivating true principle! This is why a teacher is essential in completing one's Way-karma. Even though the Abbot points it out, I still have to change it. How? By using the same method of looking within for flaws and faults – by using precepts, concentration, and wisdom until I'm pure. It's as though I never learned a thing in sixteen months of bowing! Now and tomorrow I'll talk only when it comes naturally, eat in the middle, and watch the gates.

September 4, 1978
Day 38 : To be truly free

In the afternoon the Abbot talks to a crowd of about three hundred:

"Of course there is a 'soul' within the Buddhist doctrine. We just use different terminology. We say 'eighth consciousness', or 'being between skandhas'. When one is confused, this entity is called a soul; when one is enlightened it is called the Buddha-nature. If in Buddhism we deny the existence of a soul, then there is no Buddha-nature to speak of, and what use is there of studying to become a Buddha?

"Now, rather than having just one soul, most people have three *hun* (魂) and seven *p'ai* (魄). The *hun* are *yang* and the *p'ai* are *yin*. The *p'ai* exist individually and resemble bodies of human beings, except none of them has the five faculties – one may only sport eyes, with no ears, nose, or mouth; another may have only a nose, without any of the other features, and so on. They borrow each other's faculties and together make up the entity that we mistakenly call one soul. Actually, there are ten. Sometimes when people undergo extreme terror or shock, their souls may be 'scattered', or they are 'scared out of their wits', so to speak. One or more of their ten souls may flee or become lost, and these people end up becoming very dull, or abnormal, or insane. People who haven't opened their five eyes cannot see this. But, in fact, inconceivable and uncanny things happen all the time, and if you will only believe what you personally witness, then you will miss out on a lot. Do not use the yardstick of a common person to measure the vastness of wisdom. Chuang Tzu said,

> My life has a limit, and knowledge has no limit.
> Using that which is limited to fathom what is unlimited
>   is exhausting indeed.

"Even then, most people have an insatiable craving for knowledge. However, if you haven't dealt with this question of birth and death, then no matter how much you learn, you will forget it upon your death. Take yesterday, for instance; you can't even remember what you did yesterday, so how can you remember what went on in your past life? People may go into elaborate detail learning the sciences and philosophies, yet when they die, they can't take it with them. Let's take language. Of the hundred-fifty major languages in the world, for instance, you may learn a hundred and forty-nine. Right as you are ready to master the last one, it's time for you to go. When you come back the next time, you would have forgotten, so you'd have to start all over again.

"Therefore, it is much better to have real control over your birth and death. That's being truly free. You can live as long as you wish, or when you become tired of this body you can go off to rebirth instantaneously with complete mastery. So, don't be satisfied with a little accomplishment – aim for wisdom that is boundless.

"People revolve in the six paths and have absolutely no control over their destinies.

> Out of the horse's belly, into the donkey's womb.
> How many times have you paraded before King Yama?
> From Shakra's palace on high,
> You end up at Yama's oil vat.

Every person carries on his back a 'shadow' of what he was in his past life. If you were a tiger in your past life, there will be a shadow of a tiger. Whether you were a wolf, a person, a god, a goblin, or a fox-spirit – all is revealed by the shadow you carry behind your back. Only people who have opened their five eyes can see this. But, of course, even if you can see, you don't go around disclosing other people's secrets. You can't say, 'I know you; you were such and such an animal in your previous life.' You can't do that."

In closing, the Abbot says,

"After I leave Malaysia, many people are going to scold or bad-mouth me. They don't dare do it yet, but as soon as I leave, you'll see what I mean. As for those of you who have taken refuge under me, don't beat those people up with clubs – rather, bow to them. If they say that your Master is a demon king, you should bow to them most respectfully and say, 'Yes, you're right, my teacher is a demon king. And now I, a disciple of the demon king, wish to bow to you who are not one,' then everything will be okay. In Buddhism, don't be afraid to take a loss, don't go looking for a bargain, otherwise you will not be a good Buddhist disciple. Being willing to take a loss just means being willing to benefit others. If I am of some value, then let people make use of me a little. It's okay."

Heng Sure • September 4, 1978
All kinds of weird creatures right outside the door

Big mirrors.

No more drinking milk. It has nothing that I want. It robs me of my treasures. Stay out of material goods! No more seeking! Climbing on conditions makes everyone lose faith in me. Dummy up!

The test in society is: can I be quiet? When I am quiet, I disappear, just like I should. The Abbot has opened this door – I must walk through it. Ask yourself:

"Do you want Dharani, or do you want to rap?

"Do you want this dying object, or do you want the permanent Dharma?

"Do you want the light, or do you want the self?"

The Abbot: "This is by no means a simple matter, traveling abroad. In this little place there are all kinds of weird creatures – right outside the door.

"I keep my gear all prepared – I can go to battle at any time. Not to say you should look for fights or troubles, but you should always be prepared. We are the target of every eye. Especially here at the end of the trip, it's just the time to be wary of any slip-ups or accidents. Be careful!"

September 5, 1978
Day 39 : Hoeh Beng Temple – Kuala Lumpur

At night, the Abbot delivers a light-hearted talk:

"We've gone a whole round of the country, and now we're back to Hoeh Beng Temple where we first started. During these forty days we've been treated very warmly, and I am ashamed because I haven't done much. I have sweated a lot though, both cold and hot sweat, to the point that I have lost twelve pounds already. I like this; it is better to be thin than to carry around a lot of excess weight.

"In coming over this time I've learned a great deal from all the virtuous ones and high Sanghans here, and one can say that the gods and dragons and the rest of the eightfold division have come along to protect the Dharma, thus bringing this tour to a very successful finish. Our travels have been very smooth, and even if we've encountered demons, they were friendly demons, who later were subdued by us and became our good friends.

"The causes and conditions that bring us to Hoeh Beng Temple are strange. So far, no one has scolded me right to my face, but after I leave it's not for sure what will be said. However, I look at it this way, whoever scolds me is just my Good Knowing Advisor. If they do not want me to improve, they won't say bad things about me. So I'm impelled to perfect my conduct. Now, why do people slander me? It's because they're afraid they won't have enough to eat. They're afraid that this monk will snatch away their Dharma protectors, so they launch an offensive attack first. Well, if through slandering me people can get more to eat, I consider this an indirect form of *dana* (giving) and I'm all for it. Why are people turned by states anyway? If people scold you, you become unhappy; if people praise you, you dance for joy... what type of principle is this? One that's too hard to explain!

"Now, I see that all of you are preparing for the Dharma Assembly tomorrow. With any Dharma assembly, proceed in accord with the Proper Dharma. Nothing should be haphazardly or improperly done, and then there will be a response. Don't hang on to old-time customs that are not correct – like the habit of vying to light incense. Lighting incense is an apparent dharma – an external gesture. Light up the incense of your own heart instead with true sincerity."

Later the Abbot transmits the Wisdom Mantra and two of the Forty-two Hands and Eyes:

"My gift to you in Malaysia is the gift of Proper Dharma. If you accept it, then it's your blessings. If you don't want it, that's quite all right, too."

Heng Sure • September 5, 1978
I won't let anyone else praise you

The Abbot: "They heard me praise you the other night, and they didn't think anything of it, one way or the other. But I won't let anyone else praise you to outsiders, because it sounds like we're advertising our cultivation. Now it's really fine. Nothing has to be said, because your bowing says it all – you just go and do it. It touches people and moves them to cultivate for themselves."

(Regarding Heng Sure) "He doesn't talk to anyone, especially not to women. Because of his vow power, he doesn't want to talk. People, mostly women, have tried to break his vows, but they cannot."

Heng Chau • September 5, 1978
The four borrowed elements must return

Thoughts at the Leper Colony near Kuala Lumpur.

The body is falsely set up, undependable, unreliable, and contrary. It's always going bad. Karma, the working of cause and effect, only directs how the body will go bad. For each living being it's different, because what we do and think varies. But we all go bad. The four borrowed elements must return to their source. So we turn and revolve on the wheel of life – ghosts, animals, hell beings, people, asuras, gods. "Everything that happens to us comes from what we do."

We end this (or it will end us) with a single thought. We have to recognize cause and effect and stop the turning wheel.

When you see something and you understand,
    you transcend the triple world.
When you see something and you are confused,
    then you fall under the turning wheel.

September 6, 1978
Day 40 : Your master must be a demon king!

The Abbot gives an impromptu talk:

"When you eat, you have to eat your fill; when you listen to Dharma, you have to listen your fill. Now, all of you speak better than I – my talk is very bland, like vegetables boiled in plain water, very plain. Yet, this soup is excellent for detoxifying the body. Dharma can detoxify us of our greed, anger, and stupidity. It's said,

> With a content heart, you're happy
> inside a thatched hut;
> With a still nature, even the
> roots of vegetables are fragrant.

"The problem with most Buddhists is that they want new and sensational things. 'The monk who has come from afar knows how to recite the sutras.' This may not be so. You may like to think so, but it's not for sure. Most of you have come to take a look at this delegation from America – we are a novelty. Now that you've seen this Dharma Master, you see that he's not different from any other person. I still resemble a human being. Yet, there is just one point in which I differ from most people: I don't have as many afflictions.

"If somebody says I am a demon king, then I am a demon king. How did I get this name? There used to be a disciple of mine who came often to discuss Buddhism with me. Basically, I didn't want to see anybody. So I introduced him to another Elder Dharma Master. The two of them got along capitally and soon became the best of friends.

"One day, this disciple talked to the old Dharma Master about some of his states; he said, 'Ever since I took refuge with my Master, whenever I have an illness, I dream of him and the next day my illness inevitably disappears. Also, my master appears in my house on and off, and the next moment he's vanished into thin air.' The Elder said, 'Oh, your master must certainly be a demon king! There is nobody who has spiritual penetrations in the Dharma-ending Age. If a bhikshu possesses spiritual powers, then he most certainly is a demon king.'

"That was how I got my title. By the same token, they call me one of the five great weirdos of Hong Kong. Why do they call me a freak? It's because I don't know how to climb on conditions, and this is considered to be very unorthodox; a great disgrace to the Buddhist circle. That is why people who have never met me know of me as the great demon king or as a monster. You could say that I've become famous by another route. Basically, I don't care – good names, bad names, it does not matter to me. Why spend effort on this? Good and bad is the same to me.

"Why is this called the Dharma-ending Age? Just because there is no truth. If you're a little bit true, people will feel uncomfortable. They want you to flow along with them in the dirt; they call that 'like work', one of the 'four dharmas of attraction' of a Bodhisattva. The four are:

"1) Giving. This means giving to others, not asking others to give to you. There is the giving of external and internal wealth. External wealth means giving up one's country, city, wife, and children. For example, I am now giving the City of Ten Thousand Buddhas to Buddhist disciples of the entire world, not just to my disciples. I don't have disciples – it's not that they are my disciples; they are all disciples of the Triple Jewel. So in Malaysia, I say to the several thousand who have taken refuge with me: all the highly virtuous ones are your masters. Don't make distinctions. Now I eat one meal a day and take up about eight square feet of sleeping space – why would I want such a big place as the City of Ten Thousand Buddhas all for myself? I don't want to give it exclusively to the Americans, because they don't know how to be thrifty with resources; nor do I want to give it exclusively to the Chinese; that would be selfish. I cannot give it to the Americans and Chinese only, so I've decided to give the City to the entire world.

"Giving also includes renouncing one's wife. If a layman truly understands Buddhism, he'll go as far as being able to give up his wife. Now all the wives in the assembly shouldn't get angry. If you don't want to be given away, you can leave home, too.

"Giving also means willingness to give up one's children. Have you brought forth that type of resolve? Shakyamuni Buddha lifetime after lifetime gave himself up for the sake of living beings. And true giving is joyous giving; you don't regret it after you've given.

"2) Kind words. To teach and transform, you must act as a babysitter for living beings, the way the Buddha crossed over a child with an empty fist. He saw a child drawing close to a well, about to fall into it. The Buddha's fingers curled up to form a fist and he told the child, 'Come back! I have a piece of candy in my hand for you.' The Buddha tricked the child, but he saved him from impending death. You shouldn't use kind words to butter people up. Instead you should convince them to leave confusion and return to enlightenment.

"3) Beneficial conduct. This means to do things that truly benefit others.

"4) Like work. When you want to cross people over, you should take on an appearance that is somewhat like them; in this way you can convince them bit by bit, and influence them towards the good.

"By using the Bodhisattva's four dharmas of attraction, you can attract living beings like a magnet attracts iron filings.

"Being a Buddhist means being totally true, without a single trace of falsehood. Why haven't you succeeded in your cultivation? Because your karma is a mixture of good and bad.

> If, in doing good, you wish others to know,
>> it is not true good,
> If, in doing evil, you wish others not to know,
>> it is great evil.

"Now in the past I've also done things incorrectly, but after I understood principle, I changed. I didn't want to hide behind a mask. That's why I call myself a little ant – that's a much lower status than being a demon king. I don't fear not being successful. Success and failure are one and the same to me.

"Now I am inviting all of you to come to the City of Ten Thousand Buddhas. Some of you are afraid of the suffering there. If we have rice, we'll share the rice, if we have gruel, we'll share the gruel, and if we only have water, we'll drink water. If you are not greedy, angry, or stupid, you won't have any afflictions. Afflictions come from desire; if you don't have desire, everything's okay!"

Heng Sure • September 6, 1978
There are those who know my sound

This is a very important time. We are right on the razor's edge. Battle flags are unfurled, fuses are lit, drums are beating. Smoke curls on the horizon. If we can maintain our work for another forty-eight hours, we have won.

To pull out of Malaysia with all our trophies intact will take a miracle of protection from above and complete mindfulness below. Odds are against us. The impulse to relax will be strong. It must be recognized and turned back! For me, it means to stand straight and not speak to anyone! I will see five situations that need my words. I must refuse all five – eighty-four thousand of them – let them all go. I'll give my silence to everyone! "Make a lot of gasoline for the delegation," says the Abbot.

And watch the wind of praise from the teacher/father. He is testing you both; planting the praise flowers in front of people whose approval you want. Then he watches your thoughts to see if you attach to any of it, to see if you've changed by a whisker. Don't move!

Swing your sword. Let your breath go. Watch all the gates! To arms!

The Abbot: "Here in Malaysia there are those who know my sound. My purpose in coming this time was to look around and find those who know my sound.

"You should all say everywhere that I am an artisan. Out of living flesh I create living Buddhas, Bodhisattvas, and Patriarchs. Anyone who draws near me must pass through my foundry for a time and get smelted down.

"Unite the temples. Eradicate the little places! Come together and make a big family. Put schools together, at least one per monastery. I make people, not temples."

Heng Chau • September 6, 1978
The dangers of food

Lunch at Hoeh Beng.

Rice and oil-soaked everything. The oil first took my head off. Then it clogged all the working parts and a wave of *yin* atrophy and apathy hit. Meditation was a joke — a scatter blitz. One can't run a racing car on crude oil, even if it's a crude racing car. How far away are roadside weeds, crackers, and rice, gruel, and nuts? Stream water?

Two dreams in Kuantan about dangers before leaving Malaysia:

The first was of food — hot, poison sabotage. The second was one of letting people who appeared to be close supporters (and/or sincerely interested in Dharma) in by the front door — they were crooked and after sex and money and anything else they could hustle.

Today's lunch almost wiped me out — all oily food that brought fire and desire thoughts all evening. The Abbot ate light and left the table. Last night he cryptically said, "We will be here for a couple more meals at Hoeh Beng, and then…" Why did he say that? It ties in to the dreams. Food and drink have been the cause or vehicle for a lot of problems we've faced in Asia (*yin* drinks, poisoned food, too good food, etc.).

I almost blew it with lunch today. My hunger and greed blinded me to the Abbot's caution cues. We are up against formidable odds. The Abbot only tells us how tight it was afterwards and smiles through each near disaster.

Buddhadharma has always struck me as the highest and deepest of all religions and philosophies of wisdom. The continuation of ultimate truth with the Bodhisattva ideal to help and benefit all beings was what drew me to Gold Mountain Monastery initially.

There is no body of knowledge or path of inquiry that surpasses and is not included within the principles of Buddhism. It is the ultimate penetration of and understanding of the mind and all its states.

September 7, 1978
Day 41 : Malaysian vs American Buddhism

The Abbot is asked to compare the good and bad points of Malaysian and American Buddhism,

"An obvious strong point in Malaysia is the ample supply of large lecture or convention halls in most temples and Buddhist societies here. As for something we need to amend: we should investigate the question of successorship – who is going to carry on with the mandate? Laypeople, no matter how efficient, cannot take the place of the Triple Jewel. To have a strong, healthy Buddhism we need a strong, healthy Sangha. We can't set up ludicrous examples and make ourselves the laughing stock of other people. In Penang we were taken to Guan Yin T'ing, and there, right in front of everyone's eyes, on the altar were slaughtered chicken and duck offerings – an utter disgrace!

"So, I am a people-builder, rather than a temple builder. We should unite the Sangha. In each country or province establish a branch of the central committee; in each state set up a sub-committee. This will avoid the custom of private units mushrooming everywhere, each man for himself, without any vision for the unity of Buddhism. Dharma Masters should be educated so that they are qualified to teach at all educational levels.

"The City of Ten Thousand Buddhas was not built by me; it was somehow handed over to us. If I had to build this city, I wouldn't even have enough for just the roads, let alone the electricity, the plumbing, all the buildings, or the fabulous irrigation system. Since we have such a huge headquarters in the United States, we should all share it and realize its potential."

The Abbot transmits a mantra and continues,

"This time ten members of our Association have come to Malaysia, yet this is a trick of casting away bricks and attracting jade in return. Next year for the Opening Ceremony of the City of Ten Thousand Buddhas, I want all of you to come. It's for sure that the Ten Thousand Buddhas will emit great light and shake the world. Anyone who comes will have a share of the boundless blessings... See you next year in America."

Heng Chau • September 7, 1978
The future belongs to young people

The spirit of the trip to Malaysia and *san bu yi bai* are one and the same: to bring peace and happiness to all living beings by purifying the mind of all greed, hatred, and ignorance. Within the Avatamsaka Sutra is the highest expression of this purpose, as well as a map to follow:

"If one wishes to understand all Buddhas of the past, present, and future, contemplate the nature of the Dharmarealm: everything is made from the mind alone."

World peace, family peace, personal peace, all begin with a single thought. The problems that plague Buddhism are at root the same as those that plague the world and individuals. It's called selfishness.

Buddhism's future belongs to young people, and the "times they are a changin." What Westerners want from Buddhism is the highest and purest stuff – the original teaching. They want Buddhism to be scientific and logical. They want it to surpass the foundations of Western philosophy. They want a personal involvement and direct experience. They look to Buddhism to rise above petty bickering and superstition and return directly to the source – the purification of the mind. They seek to expand their minds to embrace the limits of the Universe and to open their hearts to all living beings. They want to get enlightened in this lifetime and end wars, suffering, and disasters for all humankind. They can't be fooled or tricked by words and promises.

Many Asians don't recognize Westerners' interest in Buddhism. Westerners, disillusioned with the "good life" of Western materialism, can't see why so many Asians want it. But the gap is getting smaller, and within our lives there's going to be a lot of change, some of it painful, and a great flowering of the Proper Dharma. The seeds are in the hearts of young people today.

This trip was the first successful bridge to bring together what has divided us and to strengthen what unites us. We of the delegation have all been able to expand our hearts a little and take on the spirit of pioneers – going for the big and benefitting not just the U.S. or Malaysia, but all living beings.

This means: Buddhism can't have rich monks, ostentatious temples, lax deportment, and loose precepts. Money and sex must clearly be put down. Education must be stressed along with a deep, personal cultivation of the Way. There should be no anger, only light and big hearts.

"When the Shramana who has left the home-life puts an end to his desires and drives away his longings, he knows the source of his own mind and penetrates to the profound principles Buddhahood. He awakens to the Unconditioned, clinging to nothing, seeking nothing without."

Sutra in Forty-two Sections

"He (the Bodhisattva) is able to bear all manner of evil, and in his mind he is totally level and equal towards all beings without any agitation. Just as the earth is able to support all things, thus is he able to purify the perfection of patience."

Avatamsaka Sutra

"Don't follow me, follow yourself." In all the assemblies in forty-nine years Shakyamuni Buddha never laid down a single Dharma – just method: "Return the light and shine within." If we all can reduce our greed, anger, and ignorance, then our families, countries, and world will be happy and peaceful. The spirit of *san bu yi bai* is the same as the spirit of our trip to Malaysia – to expand the measure of our minds, change our faults, and go to the good. "Together we will go to perfect enlightenment – I hope so." "The mind is Buddha," don't seek it outside.

* * * * * * * * *

Singapore

September 8, 1978
Day 42 : Singapore Buddhist Lodge

The Abbot addresses a capacity crowd of over one thousand:

"Dear Good Knowing Advisors, this is my third visit to Singapore. The first time was twenty years ago, when I spoke at Upasaka Pitt's place, concerning the problem of left-home people and their sashes; the second time was in 1973, when I stayed at Kuang Ming Mountain, and this is my third time now. Seeing some of my old friends, Dharma Master Hui Sheng and Dharma Master Wu Fung, whom I knew from Hong Kong scores of years ago, I will tell you a story which transpired from those memorable days.

"I arrived in Hong Kong from the Mainland in 1949. From there I went to Thailand and stayed for half a year, after which I returned to Fu Rung Mountain in Hong Kong and lived at Guan Yin Cave at the back of the hill.

"Now the cave was extremely dank. There were no chairs or tables or a bed, just a big rock, on which I sat in meditation most of the time. After about half a month, upon waking up in the morning, my hands and feet were completely numb; they had absorbed too much moisture in the cave. I had to learn to move my muscles again like a little child, but even then my entire body ached with pain. I would have wanted to move elsewhere, but there wasn't any place. So, I said to myself, 'I might as well resign myself to dying in this cave.'

If you can't give up death,
     you can't exchange it for life;
If you can't give up the false,
     you'll not accomplish the true.

"So in the midst of my suffering, I realized this was what I deserved and I took it willingly.

To endure suffering is to end suffering,
To enjoy blessings is to exhaust blessings.

"I then built a little thatched hut, with sorghum stalks and some wax paper glued on the outside – it was about fifteen by fifteen feet. By now demonic obstacles arrived; somebody told the prefect at Fu Rung Mountain a false rumor, 'Tu Lun has struck it rich living in his cave. His Dharma protectors lavish on him plenty of offerings. Your temple need not feed him every day.'

"So they stopped feeding me. The person who circulated the rumor was my neighbor, a certain Dharma Master. For half a month I subsisted on what little I had inside the cave – some rice and noodles, and after that my supplies were truly exhausted. It seemed as if I was destined to starve to death inside Guan Yin cave, but I stuck to my principles,

Freezing I do not climb on conditions,
Starving I do not scheme,
Dying of poverty I do not beg.
According with conditions I do not change,
Not changing I accord with conditions.

"At this time a certain elderly layman in Hong Kong had a dream. He dreamt that Wei To Bodhisattva came to see him and said, 'Several months ago you were bitten by a dog and you still haven't recovered from your mishap. There is a Dharma Master Tu Lun at Guan Yin Cave up on Fu Rung Mountain. If you make offerings to him, your illness will most certainly be cured.' Wei To Bodhisattva then showed him a picture of me. The dream happened three times. By then the layman was convinced. He somehow amassed $70 and thirty catties of rice and carried it all the way up the mountain.

"He had just arrived at the mouth of the cave when he ran head-on into my good neighbor. My neighbor took one look at the offerings and said to the layman, 'You should hand these things over to me, I am in charge of this cave.' The layman refused. He said, 'I'm looking for a Dharma Master Tu Lun, and you are not that person.'

"They started arguing heatedly outside and created such a ruckus that I came out from the cave to see what was going on. As soon as he saw me, the layman exclaimed, 'Yes, that's him, I recognize him from the picture!'

"I explained to him, 'Since both of us live in this area, why don't you split your offerings into two. We share whatever things we get.' Only then did the layman concede to splitting up the offerings into two shares. But my good neighbor never let off. He insisted that from now on, whenever people brought me offerings, I would have to show them to him first. He took on an intense dislike of me and later on convinced the people at Fu Rung Mountain to ask me to leave.

"So I left. I moved to Hsiao Chi Huan at Ma Shan village, where there was a lot of unoccupied land, and I built a little Way Place. It was about thirty by thirteen feet. It was on a barren, steep mountainside, and I named it Hsi Le Yuan, Western Bliss Garden.

"Originally this place did not have water, but as soon as I came, a crack appeared on a rock and from it gushed forth a rippling stream. Nobody knew how it came about. Now in Hong Kong, particularly on a high mountainside, water is a prized item. Soon my neighbors had scores of buckets lined up next to my rock. Finally I had to surround the rock with barbed wire to protect the water supply, and it never exhausted itself. No matter how many people came to the Dharma assemblies, the rock kept bubbling forth with clear water."

The Abbot on a ghostly incident in Hong Kong:

"Now in Hong Kong there are wild rumors of my ghost-catching prowess. It started like this: a certain Dharma Master and seven Sanghans under him often went out to recite the sutras. One time the niece of a local businessman, Ch'an Sui Ch'ang, was possessed by a ghost. A ghost inhabited the girl's body and refused to go away. The seven monks at T'ung P'u To were invited to exorcise the ghost. They made a big ceremony of it, donning robes and sashes, reciting the Vajra Sutra, the Great Compassion Mantra, and the ten small mantras with great flourish. Yet, whenever they recited, the ghost would too. The ghost would recite its own sutra and mantras, completely defeating the monks' efforts. This persisted for a good while, until the monks were at their wits' end.

"Finally, Ch'an Sui Ch'ang came to the cave and asked me to help. Normally I did not meddle in other people's business, but since he was so insistent, I went along with him to his house.

"I did not recite any sutras, I just sat quietly next to the bed of the sick girl. In ten minutes she crept out of bed and knelt beside me.

"I asked her, 'Who are you?'

"The voice answered, 'I'm a ghost.'

"I asked, 'Why are you vexing this poor woman?'

"'Because I have affinities with her,' the ghost replied.

"The ghost asked to take refuge with the Triple Jewel. I told him that I had no wish to take any new disciples and why wouldn't he take refuge with any of the seven monks present?

"'Ha!' he said, 'Not only would I not take refuge with them; even if they came and asked to take refuge with me, I wouldn't accept them as disciples.'

"At this point I took off the prayer beads that I'd brought all the way from Manchuria and placed them on the woman's neck. The ghost immediately started whining. He said, 'Ouch, ouch, I am being roasted to death, please Dharma Master, have mercy!'

"I took the beads off and administered the refuge ceremony for him. Ever since that incident, people started calling me a *mao shan* – a Taoist – saying that my speciality was exorcising ghosts. In Malaysia I heard people introducing me as one of the Five Great Freaks, or a great demon king. They may be completely right.

Actually I don't mind, whatever name you call me, it's all the same. If I minded, would I call myself an ant, a horse, a mosquito?"

The Abbot introduces the City of Ten Thousand Buddhas:

"I've said a bunch of crazy stuff, and I know many of you don't believe me. But I most certainly believe in every single word I've uttered. Why do I want to give away such a big place as the City of Ten Thousand Buddhas and not keep it for myself? Somebody's thinking I'm a great fool. Yes. I am a fool, not smart like you. What I like to do, nobody else wants to do."

Heng Sure • September 8, 1978
They came with a vengeance today

Good news! As it stands, we will have more time to cultivate beneath the Abbot's Dharma Seat. He has observed the conditions, and we will remain in Asia for another few weeks or so. Excellent!

Heng Ch'au and I just got back our cultivation legs during our Northern Malaysia week. Now that the pressure of our first big trial is over (getting out of Malaysia intact), we can buckle down to some solid bowing and regular sitting. Kuo T'ung has found a Dharmadoor he really likes, and the three of us are working well together with *tai chi*, etc.

Like a lumpy record, I go round and round, forever out of harmony with myself. All the pieces of peace and happiness are here, but they do not yet make a perfect picture. The puzzle is incomplete. I don't recognize my career in the Way.

Instead of whimpering, I have to work harder. It is only one's own exertion that wins enlightenment. More bitterness, less ease. Dig into the sutra, the Abbot's verses, and hold your wheel, sword, light all the time. Don't let them go.

This has been the road. It will be the road. It is my path out of confusion and self.

The Abbot: "I never put my name out. I don't advertise. In general, the true ones throughout history have never been well-known. No one knows my literary works. Basically, if you have accomplishment in worldly matters, you won't be anywhere in transcendent matters.

"Cultivation must be totally natural. Even a hair's breadth of attachment will keep you from being *dz dzai*. I'm not attached to anything. Any attachment is a burden and then it's an affliction. Why do you carry that pillow around? Don't you feel it's a burden?

"In the end, any attachment will obstruct you. With any obstruction you won't get liberated. You'll be stuck there, stopped. You'll make no progress past that point. You are attached to that cushion? You feel that using it is better, but this is all in your mind. It is a Dharma attachment.

"Don't burden people. Be patient and don't seek. Just bear the discomfort."

Yesterday I asked for crackers. They came with a vengeance today. The slightest request is a leak. Cultivators cannot seek anything. There they were at lunch. Two boxes. No one served them. I resolved not to ask for them. The meal was over. Kuo Jing said, "Do you want crackers?" Too late. If I had really wanted them, this would be suffering. I shook my head "No." It was too late, and I wouldn't ask. No afflictions.

By putting them down once, I thought the test was over. I passed this test. Up in the room after lunch there came a layman carrying the two boxes of crackers. "Do you want them?"

"Not now, thanks. Serve them tomorrow when we eat." They won't be there. I won't ask for anything special again. This is going for the small. How is there any merit left for the world?

Heng Chau • September 8, 1978
To a Gold Mountain sanghan, it's a palace

Wow! Travel-scatter – the old impulse to run out through the six gates after the six dusts wells up almost unconsciously. This time, however, I know it's sure death and the effort comes forth "to return within." I can hear the verse:

> The eyes see forms, but the mind does not know.
> The ears hear dusty sounds, but inside nothing.

Singapore Buddhist Lodge.

> Everything's a test,
> To see what you will do.
> Mistaking what's before your eyes,
> You'll have to start anew.

Singapore: a spirit of free enterprise and prosperity; high energy for the checkerboard game of "Desires Five"; strong bourgeoisie à la "Protestant ethic" (Weber), only Asian style; electric buzz in the air of business and quick riches or loss interlaced with the facade of propriety and tradition.

Our base camp: first test full of all the kinds of food we prefer in abundance. Too comfortable and easy to slip and fall; rooms full of new toiletries and toys. To a layman, these are just the basic courtesies. To a Gold Mountain sanghan, it's a palace that calls out the dragons and tigers to get high and romp. Comfort equals caution.

I find myself in test alley again, only much more cautious and wary of my desire mind. Peanut butter at lunch and "fire" beans; turned them. The urge to overeat and join in the party is strong. Singapore is the kind of place the young people in the group were groomed for. It's rich in a diversity that educated, affluent "people on the climb" thrive on. Even the lodge absorbs and reflects the flavor of the "you can get anything you want" city. To a cultivator, it's a trap and a samadhi test. Inner flaws, inner desires are drawn out and revealed quickly. How pure are you? How much selfish greed remains? What turns you upside down?

Having "your merit and virtue run away" leaves a bitter, almost traumatic, after-taste. Singapore is just made from the mind – a mind of desire and ignorance; it's a lavish carnival playground and scatterland. With a mind for the Way, it's a floating mirage out of the Flower Store World – "a dream, an illusion, a bubble, a shadow." All are made from the mind.

> "According to what living beings practice in their minds, their visions of ksetras follow suit."
>
> Avatamsaka Sutra

Singapore? A fantasy island between the clouds floating in the South China Sea. A test.

"We've got everything right here!" says Kuo T'ung. So true.

> He delights in Dharma's true and actual benefits,
> And does not love the reception of desires;
> He has no greed for benefits or offerings,
> And he only delights in the Buddhas' Bodhi;
> With one mind, he seeks the Buddha's wisdom,
> Concentration undivided, with no other thought.
>
> Avatamsaka Sutra

Bitter outside, sweet inside. Sweet outside, be careful! "Do not separate from this!" It ain't Highway One and the '56 Plymouth. After Malaysia it's clear that the stakes are high and small mistakes can be fatal. "I can't relax for a minute. I don't dare," says our teacher.

So we clear the beds and soft chairs out of the room and sleep sitting up on straw mats on the floor. We do our own dirty clothes. The peanut butter and jelly gets sent back to the kitchen. "We eat

once a day and don't keep food in our rooms," Kuo K'ung relates to
our hosts.

To enjoy blessings is to end blessings;
To endure suffering is to end suffering.

We are all so dedicated to transferring to all living beings and not
climbing on conditions that we are almost allergic to good things and
comfort. We like it cold and bitter and unadorned. That's our style.
It keeps us close to the mind-ground and in touch with a heart to
save and take across others.

September 9, 1978
Day 43 : Universal Enlightenment Temple

The Abbot speaks to several young monks:

"When you're young, you should make use of your youth to the
maximum – don't waste a single minute. I've never recited the sutras
for money and I won't do it for anything, not even if I were to die of
poverty. If you like money, you shouldn't leave home. Why can't
left-home people put down fame and money?"

During evening lecture, in front of two thousand people, Heng
Ch'au talks about his experiences during Three Steps One Bow:

"The Avatamsaka Sutra says,

According to living beings' actions,
    the Buddha countries will appear.

"Your thoughts are directly linked to your world. If you have
pure thoughts, your world will be pure; if you have defiled thoughts,
your world will be defiled. Peaceful thoughts in the daytime mean
peaceful dreams at night; scattered thoughts lead to scattered dreams
or nightmares.

"On one occasion we were expecting some people to come from Gold Mountain to pick us up and take us to Los Angeles, where we see the Master once a month. I knew I should be intent on bowing, but I was so excited that whenever I got up from the ground I was scanning the highway for signs of the car. Instead of doing Three Steps One Bow, it was more like, Three Steps One Peek.

"That night I had a dream: a little child came towards me and I said, 'Oh, how cute!' It climbed onto my lap and instantly turned into a fierce iron-cast demon. It started strangling me so hard that I could hardly breathe, at which point I yelled, 'Shih Fu, Shih Fu, please help this shami out!' All of a sudden some lines from the Shurangama Mantra popped into my head. I recited them five times and the demon quickly loosened its hold over me. It fell on the ground, turning into a lifeless heap.

"When I woke up, I became aware of the true power of Mantras. I learned something: that I could rely on my master's help and mantras. Yet, I had not learned my real lesson: not to rely on outer aid. I still kept on with my false thinking. Pretty soon I had another dream in which I was again attacked by demons. This time not only one, but a whole gang of them surrounded me. As they drew nearer and nearer, I yelled, 'Shih Fu, Shih Fu, help!' No Shih Fu appeared. They were pressing closer and closer, and I was truly frightened. Right in the nick of time came the faint murmuring of the Sangha reciting a mantra. From a distance they drew near, encircled me, and I was released. Later on the Abbot appeared, but this time there was no smile on his face. He said pretty sternly, 'Kuo T'ing, if you didn't do so much false thinking, I wouldn't have to waste time in helping you out in your dreams.' From this time on I knew I have to save myself and nobody else is going to do it for me. I cannot forever seek advantages from my teacher's conditions.

"Incidentally, the Abbot knew all along. When we arrived at Los Angeles, he asked me about my dreams. I didn't even have to tell him. 'Now that you know about the dangers of false thinking, will you stop this nonsense?'"

Heng Chau • September 9, 1978
Basically we don't even want to talk

The Abbot: "When people without samadhi handle things, everyone else gets nervous and worried and then angry."

"Temple Hopping" impressions.

Precepts! We at the City of Ten Thousand Buddhas must maintain the five precepts or the Pure Land will become the Waste Land. We can tell whether the precepts are held each time we drive up to a temple – cigarette butts, pictures of nude girls, animals on altars, loose and loud talk, groups sitting around rapping and joking, men and women left-home people rubbing up against each other – no clear separation. It's all made from the mind – if the mind is off an inch, no matter how much money or temple bricks you have, it still isn't a Way-place.

The Abbot: "They're *san bu yi bai*. They don't indulge in gossip and small-talk. They just want to talk about Dharma and cultivation." (to a monk)

Basically we don't even want to talk – just cultivate. Cultivation talks for itself. Talking for itself (i.e., talking for the sake of talking) is not cultivation.

I have to learn Chinese: I asked for a mirror and got a cup of milk. Today laundry soap and a thermos of hot water involved over twenty people running for plastic pails, one hundred pounds of soap, tea cups, and two kettles of hot water.

September 10, 1978
Day 44 : I tear down temples – the small ones

The Abbot about sitting pillows:

"The reason you people use a pillow while sitting is that you rely on something outside of yourself. I see you doing it in America – even when the seats are cushioned with rubber foam, everybody still sticks a pillow underneath his bottom. This is called attachment to Dharma. When I was young, I trained myself so that I could sit anywhere on the ground without any support. At Guan Yin Cave I sat on a rock for months. There's nothing you can't do, unless you don't want to apply effort.

"If there is attachment, there is a burden. With even a single trace of attachment to Dharma, you're stuck. You're suspended in that space, you can't move on and improve. I've seen all of you become attached this way, so today I must tell you. The same attachment extends to everything else: food, sleep, clothes, etc. All dharmas should be cultivated naturally, without any force or artificiality.

"Now I know that my body deserves no blessings. A bit too much of nourishing food – even an extra morsel – my body can't take it. Even when you have enough Way virtue, you shouldn't make others serve you; how much the less when you don't even have any! I see that some of you allow others to do your laundry for you. These people aren't paid to serve us; we are not living in a hotel. I wash my own clothes, even at Gold Mountain or the City of Ten Thousand Buddhas. Why? Because I don't want to trouble people. That's just another way of piling up your debts. Eventually you have to pay it all back and that's not a lot of fun. If we are true Buddhist disciples, we should always set an example for everyone and not make people cater to our comforts."

And now, turning to the two monks:

"Of course, you can't wash your clothes right in front of people, otherwise they will grab them from you. See, it is discretion in these cases that is the high art within Buddhism. Have any of you ever seen me do my own laundry?"

In the evening, the Abbot speaks to about two thousand people:

"I am one of shallow learning and virtue. So when I speak crazy words, not many people like to hear them. However, I feel that the move to rejuvenate Buddhism is every Buddhist's responsibility. The mistake we all make is being selfish and self-seeking, on the one hand telling other people about the Bodhisattva conduct, on the other being selfish. This selfishness is worse than a festering cancer within Buddhism. There is no more unity and all-embracing vision. Everyone vies to build impressive temples: you build a fifty-foot temple, I'll build a fifty-one footer, he builds a fifty-two footer, and so on until we have temples that are thousands of feet high. Yet, these temples are empty; nobody lives or cultivates in them. They obstruct empty space. Therefore, when people ask me what I do, I reply, 'I am a temple dismantler!' (loud applause)

"What temples do I tear down? Just the little ones built exclusively for one Sanghan only. I tear down the little temples so that these people will move into the big Way places and live together under the same rules. Why are small temples not desirable? Because within them one can live without any restraint or discipline. You easily become too comfortable. You become your own boss, lording over everything, too comfortable with sleeping, eating, wearing clothes, to the point that you forget to cultivate. All you think about is how to butter up more Dharma protectors for offerings.

"This custom greatly scatters the strength and unity of Buddhism. Some laypeople are under the impression that acting as a Dharma protector for one Sanghan member results in limitless merit and virtue. This is a mistake. You protect their Dharma to the point that they run back to laylife. Then your loss is great indeed. Left-home people may get so comfortable that in the end they will not be comfortable at all. (cheers from the young, smiles and approving nods from the older crowd)

"Now it is my suggestion – I say 'suggestion' only, so if you don't like it, there's no need to get angry – that Sanghans should not hoard any private assets. Once Sanghans have money, they give rise to false thoughts, and that leads to endless afflictions. Once ignorance flares up, people may do a lot of upside-down things that are not in accord with Dharma. If you don't have any money, you may still be okay. Once you have some, then you have the means to go wild.

"Wake up quickly, my friends! I speak not for myself, but for everyone. If I have even one single hair of selfishness within me, I vow to forever stay in the hells. Now you think: am I so stupid to make such a vow if I didn't mean it?

(Heated applause. By now some irate Dharma Masters stand up and stomp out.)

"Don't laugh, all of you; this is no laughing matter. Buddhism is about to perish, and we have to quickly find ways to save it. You should take the rise or fall of the Dharma as your very own responsibility. Don't keep on passing the buck. Don't be telling other people to give and yet give nothing yourself. Just think, you can't take this money with you to your grave. You came with nothing, you will go with nothing. When you still have the time, why don't you create some great merit instead? Don't be stingy! You have to give things up in order to have true attainment.

"This afternoon, when I was talking to the Buddhist Youth Association, I said, 'I never accept any private offerings.' Somebody doesn't believe this. They say, 'We see all those red packets you take in every day, and you say you don't accept private offerings?' Since the day I left home, whenever I have been given private offerings, I have always stuffed them into the public alms box, and only when nobody could see me. When I came to America, my American disciples wanted to follow suit. Some of them keep the precept of not handling money, many eat once a day at noon, and some sleep sitting up. Now, I don't know why, but this morning somebody brought up a whole tray of bread, butter, milk, and fruit into my room. I didn't know whether to laugh or cry, all I could say was, 'No, no, I don't want it.' I don't know who conceived of this idea. Perhaps they wanted to test me out, to see whether this Dharma Master really adheres to his rules, or whether he can be persuaded to take a nibble.

"I had three conditions set up from my days in Manchuria. The first is, 'Freezing I do not climb on conditions.' All of you rich people don't worry. I guarantee that I won't have designs on you or butter you up. If we want money, we needn't have left the home life. The second condition is that I don't recite the sutras for money. No wonder people call me a weirdo: I'm in complete opposition to what most Sanghans do. The third condition is that I don't want any post, like head of the assembly or head prefect, etc. At Nan Hua Monastery the Elder Hsu Yun requested that I be head of the assembly, and at first I refused. He said, 'If you young people don't do anything, all the work would fall on us old folks.' Then I had no choice but to accept the appointment."

Heng Sure • September 10, 1978
Your balance sheet must be clean

The Abbot: "Wherever we go, we can move rocks and wood – I'm convinced – because we want to go towards the good on all sides, at every hand.

"When you talk, don't embroider. When you paint pictures of people, don't draw in their guts. Just speak the essentials.

"Any service you impose on other people becomes a debt. It will be repaid in the future. Your balance sheet must be clean. We must not give people trouble. We are Buddhists and we don't rely on anyone else's help. I never feel I have the Way-virtue to use other people. If I had it, even less would I ask favors.

"You use your effort only on food, don't you? (after the cracker story). I eat three bowls of rice each day and then stop. I could eat ten or twenty with no trouble – it would feel just the same to me – but I choose not to."

Every day I false-think of the dragon car and the quiet highway. Touring is okay, hearing the Dharma is fine, getting constant teaching is strenuous and rewarding (and frustrating). Failing to give my best is a thorough bummer.

Heng Chau • September 10, 1978
Don't you understand the significance of this?

The Abbot: "With too much comfort, how can you cultivate? When cultivating you can't impose upon others, even if you have the Way-virtue. Don't climb on conditions! Don't even let them see or know when you wash your own clothes. Cultivation is just that kind of discretion."

The way to cultivate the food trip is to develop *gung fu* (skill) to the point that you can turn every state, "Clinging to nothing within, seeking nothing without." It should be that every meal is "level and equal" and there should be no way that anyone can tell whether you "prefer" this over that or have "special" likes and dislikes.

The Abbot: "It's okay not to eat sugar now. But ultimately (in the end) you're going to have to come back and break through what you can't take (the attachment). With even a hair's breadth of attachment to any dharma you can't attain *dz dzai* (comfort)."

There's no such thing as learning without cultivating. Although we may think we understand, it's not ours until we swallow it ourselves. One doesn't learn any more or less by climbing on his teacher's conditions. Without hard work, there's no benefit – the Dharma gift isn't recognized. If we work hard, a single glance from the Master can bring a small enlightenment. If we are lazy, an entire two-hour lecture is like listening to the wind.

The Abbot accords and meets us half way. He never forces or resists anything. That's the Tao.

We know the use of what is, but few know the utility of what is not.

Tao Te Ching

Verses come from the Avatamsaka that keep us from getting lost:

> I don't rely on form, I'm not attached to feelings,
> I am not turned upside-down by thoughts.
> I don't do actions; I don't seek consciousness.
> I forsake the six places.
>
> I do not dwell in mundane dharmas,
> My joy is in leaving the world;
> I know that all dharmas are like empty space,
> They come from nowhere.
>
> They are neither produced nor destroyed,
> They lack true reality;
> I am not defiled by attachment to them,
> I leave behind all views and distinctions...
>
> He sees all forms up to and including all tactile dharmas,
> Be they attractive or ugly,
> He produces neither love nor disdain for them.
> His mind achieves *dz dzai*.
>
> He makes no mistakes, his mind is vast, big, and pure.
> He is happy, blissful, apart from all worry and vexation.
> His mind (heart) and his will are soft and flexible.
> All his organs (roots) are clean and cool.
>
> The Bodhisattva's practices are all like shadows.
> He brings forth the unattached pure Dharma eye
>   which looks upon the uncreated vast state.
> He realizes its still nature; he understands
>   that all dharmas are non-dual.
> He attains the real mark of dharmas...

The Bodhisattvas inhabit the world,
And they are not attached to any dharmas,
  either inside or outside;
Like the wind which travels through space
  without obstruction,
The Great Knight's concentration is also like this.

Real freedom and independence with no fear or anxiety comes from mastering the rules. The highest *gung fu* is that of dwelling in constant peace with body, mouth, and mind. Pure karma, a clean balance sheet, is the only real peace and happiness. Perfect cause and effect down to each thought and what problems would we have?

No karma and no affliction,
Without possessions and without a dwelling-place,
He neither illumines, nor does he practice anything.
He travels in level equality through the world.

Avatamsaka Sutra

The Abbot: "The most important thing to the group is that no one should be jealous and obstructive. If that happens, then the delegation is dead, e.g., we should all recognize the importance of what we're doing. There's no rain during Dharma lectures – don't you understand the significance of this?"

September 11, 1978
Day 45 : Don't just build temples; build schools

The Abbot announces in a morning meeting:

"Yesterday, while talking to the Youth Buddhist Association, I told them that after I die I want my body to be burnt. My bones and ashes should be ground to a powder, rolled up with flour, sugar, or honey, and fed to the ants. Why? Because I've called myself an ant, and I have great affinities with ants. After having made a meal out of me, they should quickly resolve on Bodhi.

"Now that I've made this decision, make sure that you follow my instructions. When the time comes, I don't wish to leave any trace behind.

"Sweep clean all dharmas, separate from all marks.

"I don't wish to leave a flesh body behind like the Sixth Patriarch or Dharma Master Tzu Heng. I don't want any stupas or memorial hall built in my memory."

The Abbot then explains the reason why he does not wish to leave any marks upon his death…

"Why do I specify this request? Because not many people believe in my giving away the City of Ten Thousand Buddhas to the entire world. They can't believe that there's someone whose only aim is to benefit all beings. I've given the City of Ten Thousand Buddhas to everyone in the world, not just to Americans or Chinese, not just to Buddhists, but to all living beings, people of all other religions as well. I've observed the causes and conditions of Buddhism, and only through a dynamic act of selfless giving can Buddhism be saved. Otherwise it will surely die. So in the future, nobody can lay private claims on the City of Ten Thousand Buddhas or any part of it. It will forever remain public property of World Buddhism… What do you think?

"The only people who are allowed to run the City are people who are selfless, people who truly practice the Bodhisattva conduct of benefiting all. It cannot be used for private gain or benefit. I told you last night that if I have a single hair's worth of selfishness I'm willing to forever stay in the hells. Always give away the good things to others, don't hoard them for yourself. Don't seek name or recognition. And above all don't be jealous and obstructive. Whoever is better than I, I respect that individual but will never obstruct him."

The Abbot about an earlier incident where some Sanghans walked out and the laypeople cheered:

"The cheering was also not in accord with Dharma – I told people that this is no laughing matter. The very survival of Buddhism is at stake. Not only should Sanghans not keep private assets, even laypeople who dedicate their lives to Buddhism shouldn't keep private assets. Otherwise a very imbalanced situation will appear with all the money concentrated in the laypeople's pockets. This campaign against burning incense and paper is just paving the initial steps of the revolution. As we gather momentum there will be a much wider sweep of things. The custom of reciting the sutras for money will be abolished, for example. Right now this ritual serves as bread and butter for most of the Sanghans in Asia, plus a lot of lay Buddhists as well. But the time isn't ripe; if I were to tell them now, they wouldn't be able to accept it.

"The Sanghans in China used to be largely uneducated. For all the wealth each temple amassed, there were no Buddhist schools – no elementary schools, no high schools, not even one Buddhist university throughout the entirety of China. I've seen temple treasuries loaded with gold bars, with their weight in tons in fact, yet people were selfish, hoarding it for themselves, not spending it to help Buddhism thrive. That is why I say I am not a temple builder. Yes; I am an artisan, but instead of working in gold, wood, clay, or stone, I hone Buddhas, Bodhisattvas, Patriarchs, and Arhats out of living flesh.

"All our efforts should be expended on education. If you Americans are going to build in the future, don't just build temples; build schools. Every school should be equipped with a large lecture hall which can be used for all purposes: worshipping, reciting, Dharma assemblies, and lectures. Building educational institutions is my wish. No matter where I go, I speak from my true heart, and there's no way people won't be moved. Not only people, even wooden stumps and rocks will bend to the sound of true Dharma."

Bhikshuni Hui Shen about seeing the degenerate state of Asian Buddhism and the disorganized Sangha:

"If we are selfish and squabble among ourselves, or cater only to appearances with no thought for actual cultivation, how can we merit the name of left-home people?"

"When we see these beings suffering so miserably, how can we fail to bring forth compassion? I'm just a Bhikshuni with little status, yet for as long as I have a single ounce of strength I must dedicate it to the revival of the Dharma."

The Abbot at a refuge ceremony of over six hundred:

"It's said that in a single day it is easy to sell ten bushels of the false, yet in ten days it is hard to buy one bushel of truth. Many people believe in the false, and very few believe in the true. This is due to our habit from beginningless kalpas, that of mistaking suffering as bliss. Everything I say to people is false. Why? Because you cannot utter the truth. All marks are false and empty, all words are false and empty. When the point is reached that the path of words is cut off, and the mind's activities cease – only there can you find truth. Yet right within the false is the truth, and right within truth is the false. True and false do not obstruct one another, they are interpenetrating.

"Also, truth is not true of itself, and the false is not false of itself; rather, it is living beings who make it either true or false. Living beings are just Buddhas, sages, and gods. Living beings are temporarily attached to confusion and turn their backs from enlightenment. Once the confusion is peeled off, enlightenment is revealed therein: it is at no other place. Disregarding our family treasure we have become prodigal sons, willingly shuffling waste and collecting garbage. Wouldn't you say this is a pity?

"If you want to find the truth, just don't do anything false. This means in every gesture or word, do not be false.

The path comes from practice;
Without practice there is no path.
Virtue is cultivated;
Without cultivation there is no virtue.

Merit established on the outside,
Virtue is developed inside.
If you establish merit on the outside,
Your virtue inside will abound and you will be filled
  with your original wisdom and Dharma bliss.

The T'ang poet, Han Yu, said in a few lines from his essay, The Original Way:

Humaneness is universal affection; righteousness is appropriateness in action; going from here to there is the Path; virtue is contentment with oneself and not relying on outer resources; the heart is the root of humaneness, righteousness, principle and wisdom. This produces a glow that naturally flushes one's skin, lights up one's arms, and infuses one's four limbs. The four limbs thus speak without saying a word.

In fullness there is beauty; in fullness and light there is greatness; greatness transformed is sageliness; sageliness which knows itself becomes godliness...

"Han Yu's essay can be applied to cultivation. When you have universal concern for all, just this is humaneness; if you behave properly for every occasion, that is righteousness; going from here to there is traveling on the Way; possessing virtue just means embracing loyalty, humaneness, reason, and wisdom. Then a glow will exude from your entire body. People who cultivate have a lot of light about them. The harder you cultivate, the more light you have and your light speaks without need for words. When you truly fortify yourself with Way-virtue, you'll achieve beauty, greatness, sageliness, and godliness.

"When you are in total communion with these states, you have achieved your heart's desire, without having in the least bit transgressed the law of heaven and nature. Confucius put it this way:

> At fifteen I resolved on learning. At thirty I stood firm.
> At forty I was no longer confused. At fifty I understood the
> decree of heaven. At sixty my ear was an organ for the
> reception of truth. At seventy I could do whatever my heart
> wanted and yet not transgress propriety.

"When Confucius said that at sixty his ear was the organ for the reception of truth, it meant that whatever he heard was in accord and was pleasant. Only at seventy was he able to freely do what his heart desired and yet never transgress the proper. What a liberation that is! It is just recovering the spontaneous, divinely innocent quality in our nature. People who wish to study Buddhism should first learn to be good people; do not do things that only benefit yourself but harm others.

"Now Tao Yuan Ming, the famous fourth century pastoral poet, was famous for his lofty character. He gave up a high governmental post because he would not bend to protocol and bureaucracy, but preferred to live blissfully in communion with Nature. In the Ode of Return he sings:

> The fields have grown wild.
> Why do I not return?
> My heart has been enslaved by my body,
> How can I not lament in lonely sorrow!
> Understanding my past faults,
> I know that I can make amends for the future.
> Not having gone too far down the deviant path,
> I awaken to today's rights and yesterday's wrongs.

"This poem is well-tuned to the Buddhist's heart. When we say, 'The fields have grown wild,' it can refer to our mind-ground which is thick with the weeds of ignorance. We should quickly return to the Western Land of Ultimate Bliss. Then we can turn the boat around and save the beings in the Saha world. Our mind has become a captive of our body and we have no real mastery over things. This is, of course, a state worthy of remorse. However, upon understanding mistakes we've made in the past – as Confucius said, 'Having reached fifty, I know my errors of the past forty-nine years' – we should then look forward to the future and make amends. There's still hope. What's right today is studying the Buddhadharma; what was wrong yesterday was throwing your life-force away. Another poem says,

> If you do not seek the Great Way
>   to leave the path of confusion,
> Despite blessings and worthy talent
>   you're still not a great hero.
> A hundred years is but sparks struck from a rock.
> A body is a bubble bobbing in water
> Wealth will be left behind; it doesn't belong to you.
> Offenses follow you and it's hard to cheat yourself
> With gold piled high as a mountain,
> Can you bribe impermanence when it comes?

"If you do not seek to leave the dust, however many talents and worldly skills you possess will still be in vain. Don't be too smart for your own good. Why don't you use your intelligence to cultivate instead? Even with profuse erudition and a stomachful of learning, you still don't figure as a great hero. A great hero is one who transcends the performance of his peers; he has impressive vision and prowess. Time flies by in a flash. Don't think this money, this pretty wife, these houses and cars are yours – you can't take them with you. When the time comes for you to see King Yama, you can't bribe the ghost of impermanence, even with your mountains of gold and silver."

The Venerable Master holds a refug

...eremony on the last night in Singapore

Heng Chau • September 11, 1978
But I know what would've happened

My contact with women before the resolve for Bodhi was filled with a lot of confusion and pain. My contact with women after bringing forth the mind for the Way has involved a life and death struggle. My vows and Way-karma do not allow me to be casual about this – the slightest mistake brings heavy retribution. Bad dreams, sickness, and near-death are the personal losses. On the larger scale, I don't know, but the Abbot has clearly said that the mishaps and bad weather, etc., we confront on *san bu yi bai* come from our false thoughts. So it's safe to assume that there's a lot at stake, and I had better put down this *mau bing* once and for all. My own life is one thing, but the score of the vows of *san bu yi bai* is another.

This whole trip has been one purge and sickness after another. If I stop to think about any of the difficulty I've gone through since starting to cultivate, it could really be a bummer. But, I know what would've happened if I hadn't cultivated – sad and tragic beyond words. So there's a deep feeling of peace and "everything's O.K." in all this suffering. "Big disasters become little ones, and little disasters disappear."

September 12, 1978
Day 46 : He is singly the most forceful personality

The Abbot speaks highly of Professor Yu Kuo K'ung after his departure in the morning:

"He is singly the most forceful personality in this group. He has a vast, broad mind; everything is open with him. This is the uprightness of a great hero who works for the benefit of all. In all things you should keep your eye on the entire picture, the larger scope. There's no room for petty concerns about one's own benefit. Don't be one who thrives on eating, sleeping, putting on clothes, and spends the rest of the time being jealous and obstructive."

The Abbot on the excellent weather:

"For all the days we've been here it has not rained once before or after the lecture when people are coming and going. If you still do not understand to what an incredible degree the gods, dragons, and others of the eightfold division are supporting the Dharma, then you have really missed the message."

Heng Chau • September 12, 1978
Bitten by a tiger, he now knows fear

All this sickness has brought a lot of understanding:

1) My desire for women, arising from ignorance, is the same as sure death and blinds me to seeing it like it really is. "He has lived in the mountains and been bitten by tigers. So now he knows fear."

2) Food – watching it turn to a foul pile of liquid in the toilet minutes after it enters my mouth is an eye-opener. "Three inches past your tongue and you couldn't stand to eat it." Really empty, the same as sexual desire – going for the small.

3) Cause and effect is for real and not off by a hair. Each cause must be clean or for sure you'll take a loss. True emptiness is just pure karma. It has come down to millimeters in a casual and/or unchecked false thought to sickness.

4) This is a happy way of life for all of us: living out of packs and bags, free to travel whenever conditions are ripe, eating little, sleeping little, working hard without and turning the light deep within. Nothing is predictable. No routine gets established except precepts and our vows. With no anger or grudges, soft and pliant hearts, we polish the dust off our wisdom mirrors – mutual support without attachment, closeness without love (desire). There's no time to remember yesterday – too busy to worry about tomorrow. We're

young warriors for peace and happiness, inexperienced but with resolve and true vision.

The Abbot patiently advises and takes the brunt of enemy attacks. He does the dirty work at night while everyone else sleeps. "Don't follow me, follow yourself! Use your own wisdom."

The Abbot's deportment and behavior are flawless, friendly and open, smiling yet without errors or slips – an invisible vajra shield; mine is visible and plastic. He sees who to talk with and who to avoid, what children to play with and which ones carry hexes. *Dz dzai* comes with no ignorance; it's a natural state of being one with spiritual powers, and spiritual power has something to do with seeking nothing.

> The manifestation of spiritual power,
> This is called the Buddha.
> In all the three periods of time,
> You can seek, but there is nothing at all which exists.
>
> Avatamsaka Sutra

* * * * * * * * *
Thailand

September 14, 1978
Day 48 : We've brought you a present

In the evening, the Abbot speaks to a crowd of about seventy:

"This is my third visit to Thailand, and I will first introduce myself. In Malaysia I'm known as one of the five great freaks of Hong Kong. Now, as to why people think me so bizarre I don't know, perhaps because I eat one meal a day, or because I wear my precept sash at all times. But I do these things in order to manifest the appearance of a bhikshu, and in no way am I trying to set up a special style of my own. Others say that I am a *mao shan*, a Taoist ghost-exorciser. This rumor was started by a certain self-acclaimed leader of the Secret School in Hong Kong whom I've never had the pleasure to meet. Perhaps he didn't dare to call himself a monster, so he has chosen to call me one instead.

"However, in coming to Asia this time, we've brought you a present. I've paved a new road that starts from America, and which spans the entirety of Malaysia, Singapore, Thailand, Hong Kong and Taiwan. Completing the full circle, it unites the East and West. I often call myself a road, and any being can walk over me. I also call myself an ant, a horse, a mosquito. No matter how many names I have, they are all false anyway.

"Now tonight I am supposed to speak on Buddhism in America, and I'll sum it up for you in one word: the religion of stupidity. Why? Just look at these monks prostrating themselves once every third step. They bow up a big sweat, and every day – be it rain or shine – they keep on bowing. Just think, if this is not stupid then what is it? And yet,

If you can't give up death,
　　you can't exchange it for life.
If you can't relinquish the false,
　　you can't accomplish the real.

Cultivating till you're like an idiot
　　is just the wonderful;
Only when your learning approaches
　　stupidity is it truly rare.

To endure suffering is to end suffering,
To enjoy blessings is to exhaust your blessings.

"If you call yourself a Buddhist disciple, why can't you endure the least bit of suffering? You tell others to give, but you yourself do not give; you tell others to cultivate, but you yourself do not cultivate; that's called talking about food but not getting your fill. Don't spend your time in the samadhi of bantering. Also, in cultivation one shouldn't be moved by any state, whether pleasant or unpleasant. If upon meeting a pleasant state you are happy, or upon meeting an unpleasant state you're sad, then you are just being turned."

Heng Sure • September 14, 1978
A new self-image without a mouth

The Abbot: "See, I'll show you how to do it. You take the empty bowl and put it over the full one so that it covers it. Then you can invert them and nothing falls out, it all stays inside. Do you understand?"

This was not a lesson in table etiquette. The Abbot was explaining how to be in the midst of the worldly dust and not lose your essence. The secret: cover the full bowl with an empty bowl, i.e., don't do any false-thinking, don't occupy your mind with any thoughts. Let your empty mind cover your full center. Then you can flow with any situation, merge with a crowd of juice-hungry demons and keep on smiling without losing anything.

I am training a new self-image that does not have a mouth. The energy circuit no longer exits here. My mouth is by-passed and the spark moves right on by.

The Bangkok vow: no more words will come from my mouth. I took six weeks to find the strength.

> With one mind undivided, he seeks the
>   Buddhas' wisdom.
> He does not love the reception of desires,
> He is not greedy for offerings.
>
> In all worlds in the ten directions,
>   he stops nowhere, he relies on nothing.
> He seeks not even life itself
>   or any of the other many dharmas.
> Nor does he falsely give rise to discriminations.
>
> Avatamsaka Sutra

The Abbot: "Gold is best for Buddha images. Silver is also good, or copper/brass mixed with gold. These are all better than wood or clay. In general, use something that is valuable. Use what you are most unable to part with and make a Buddha out of just that."

Heng Chau • September 14, 1978
Fierce, powerful, and hard to subdue

Bangkok.

Hot, humid – there's tension in the air – a feeling of Mordor, dark vapors, closed in and suffocating. People seem very nervous with no spark of joy in their hearts. Traditional society and Buddhism are relics here, like homeless ghosts wandering the streets and countryside where once was their palace. Now it's neglected – in ruins. The mind of materialism fills the air with bad *chi* wherever we go. Greed fights with greed and hatred boils over, spilling ignorance and bad karma, filling the air, soaking through buildings, skin. This exists everywhere in the world today.

A shadow hangs over the world, but there's a new sun in the smelting. We are in transition. Within our lives we will see many catastrophes and a lot of suffering. But the Dharma won't be allowed to die. When it's time, it will blaze forth with unchanging brilliance and after-the-rain purity. The storm clouds build and pass; the sun doesn't move.

I've seen this vision and dreamed of what's to come. I need to work harder and be truer. When has the vessel ever been worthy of the jewel? Soon all of us will be doing what we do best – to try to make vessels strong and clean enough to guard the treasure.

Turning sexual desire is slow and takes the most concentration and effort. Seeing through food, fame, wealth, and sleep are difficult, but not like this. They still return and kindle a flame if I am casual or think I've got something, but I can subdue them. I barely have a handle on the sex demon, though. It's almost comical to watch my eyes catch passing women. Only when everything is seen as level and equal, still and empty – when no thing is singled out over another – only then is desire and longing subdued. "The dragons crouch and the tigers curl up."

When we wrestle with dragons and subdue tigers in constant sport, ghosts cry and spirits wail, in strange magical transformations.

Master Hsuan Hua

Why doesn't *san bu yi bai* go sightseeing?

1) All our lives we have chased after the "sights." This time is dedicated to concentrated hard work to the extreme for all living beings.

2) "Everything is made from the mind alone." Whatever we see is just a mirror of our thoughts. No two people see the same – each sees according to what is practiced and to his basic attitude. Hungry people look the world in one way, happy we look at it in another. In love men and women look at it in one way, having been cheated or when facing death love looks different – sick, healthy, rich or poor. Ultimately, how is it? "An illusion, a bubble, a dream, a shadow." No matter where we go and what sights we see, we're always looking at ourselves.

There's a new Pope. He faces the same problems that his predecessors faced: the moral questions, the same ones we all face – divorce, abortion, contraception vs. lasting marriages, no killing, no extra-marital sex, etc.

The world is infatuated with materialism to the extreme. Call it greed run wild. The "haves" want to hoard, the "have nots" want their share, and everyone wants more. This is the Age of Desire. In no other time in history have so many wanted so much. Desire for food, wealth, for sex, and sleep, and fame are universal. The traditional laws and moral codes that once contained this greed have gone out with the horse and monarchies. It's everyone for himself. "Blood is thicker than water" has been replaced by "Money is thicker than blood."

All desire is just sexual desire. In Buddhism sexual desire is represented by tigers and dragons: fierce, powerful, and hard to subdue – able to tear you to shreds. All the manifold headaches and problems stem from sexual desire.

Penetrating the phenomenal or conditional world takes concentration power, i.e., strong will and a disciplined mind. Thus, the Threefold Non-Outflow study of Morality, Concentration, and Wisdom. Desire can't be suppressed or denied. It has to be transformed and returned to its root: ignorance. What kind of ignorance? The ignorance of self.

Wisdom is just the recognition of the truth of no self. With no self, what problems could there be? With no self, who is there to worry or fear? With no self, what is there to seek or want? All the problems of the world come from the false self.

Here is Buddhism's contribution to the world religions and world peace: a living tradition of eighty-four thousand different methods which allow people to attain deep and liberating wisdom. Buddhism has an arsenal of weapons for taming tigers and dragons. It's the next step up from morality. If Catholics and Buddhists could combine their strong morality with Ch'an meditation, the Heavenly Demons and Mara would for sure tremble and stop bothering the world.

There's a common phrase in anthropology: "Some cultures call themselves polygamous and others say they're monogamous. But adultery is universal." The point being that the behavior of cheating is common to all peoples. Our actual practices are much the same; what is different is the names we tag onto them.

It's the same with religion. There's as much superstitious belief and practice in "Buddhism" as in any other religion. Buddhist monks and nuns stain themselves with wealth, politics, and sex as much as those of other faiths. Following or ignoring the rules crosses religious boundaries, and so does confusion or understanding. It all comes down to a simple formula: practice true principle. This is the shared source of all religions – the root-nature of all peoples. We should find the pearl within and mutually shine on each other.

September 15, 1978
Day 49 : Universally Calm Temple

The Abbot on private property:

"There are many people within Buddhism who try to steal a bell while stopping up their own ears. This is called cheating yourself and cheating others. Not only are you not reliable in your cultivation, you put up a front and influence others in Buddhism to do likewise. No wonder outsiders are not inspired to bring forth respect or faith in our religion. Knowing this I am determined to change what is wrong, and I must start with myself.

"Ever since the day I left home, I have never hoarded private assets. Whenever people gave me offerings it all went to the central funds of the temple. I never harped about the money; whatever policy suited the majority was fine with me.

"The City of Ten Thousand Buddhas is ready-made. It has about seventy buildings with first-class facilities: lecture halls, study rooms, conference rooms, plus ample space for a lot of expansion. That's why I want to give it to the whole world.

"The reason why I urge Sanghans to give up holding private assets is that once you have money, trouble arises. You start to eat, drink, and play as you wish, and many are lured back to laylife. If monks don't hoard private property it won't be as easy for them to go astray. Instead of building temples, let us build schools. Because we neglected education in the past, we have not been able to plant roots of faith within people's hearts. With this fault in its foundation, Buddhism could not withstand stormy weather. From now on, if we fortify our educational system, build elementary schools, high schools, and universities, then young people will develop a first-hand understanding of the Dharma.

"This is why next year we will hold an International Buddhist Convocation at the City of Ten Thousand Buddhas. The purpose is to elect a head of the Buddhist Central Assembly, as well as to draft the constitution and bylaws by which all Sanghans can model their lives. Now, most people do not believe that I really want to give the City of Ten Thousand Buddhas to the whole world. I've always been stupid like this. However, sooner or later they'll have to believe.

"Every Buddhist should take up the responsibility of propagating the Dharma and not push it onto someone else's shoulders. There is nothing wrong with Buddhism per se; however, we ourselves as Buddhist disciples are to blame for our present problems. Buddhist disciples should daily reflect: what contribution have I made towards Buddhism today? If we haven't made any, we should be ashamed and quickly change!"

Heng Sure • September 15, 1978
Everyone will get to bathe in their light

The Abbot: "...and I heard from what you said that you weren't moved by what went on at Pu Jing's place. This is a good sign – it's a stage of cultivation that you have to go through. You weren't turned by the state. You are concentrating."

Heng Sure: "Shih Fu, I haven't seen anyplace that I thought was special. I like our car best, I really miss it." (laughter)

The Abbot: "I know for a fact that all the Buddhas and Bodhisattvas will release great lights when we open the light at the City of Ten Thousand Buddhas next year. It's going to be a big affair – everyone will get to bathe in their light."

Poisoned by lunch: Oil, garlic, MSG. It's been two days now – each bow is a blackout blitz. Bow down and start the newsreels – funny head movies. The Abbot is teaching me not to be attached to anything. So, okay, sometimes it just doesn't go your way.

"Why be hung-up on food? Suppose you were a Theravada monk and begged for every bite? You wouldn't know about today's meal until you went walking. Tomorrow would be the same. Certainly you will be fed, pure chance determines what it will be. Yes you will eat; no you don't know what. As a Mahayana Bhikshu you have never gone hungry. There is always food available for your one meal. Why think about it? How much the less need you worry about it."

Heng Chau • September 15, 1978
You should be able to tell by now

Riding in the car, listening to the Abbot say how stupid he was, it finally sank in – that's it! Everyone else is so smart: seeking this and that for self-benefit, making sure not to take a loss or give up too much, keeping a "little" nest egg, etc. The Abbot lives what I've only read of in the Avatamsaka Sutra – he's totally selfless and unattached, transferring all merit and virtue, not stained by worldly dharmas – *dz dzai.*

How stupid! To do what we all dream of and cherish – to really do it, like a child completely trusting and unafraid. Mind blowing! There's no one else in all the world as stupid as this.

The more external props used, the more confused and scattered the effort. Scattered and attached to form and sound, there's no penetration, and the Wheel of Life turns and turns and drags us back.

I've felt more at home and inspired in the back seat of the Plymouth than in the most exquisitely adorned temples of Southeast Asia. The temples in Asia are for "Buddhist Monopoly" and ego thrones, or for offering caches, or hanging out. We've seen only one or two temples where anyone was cultivating the path that Shakyamuni Buddha recommended.

Wan Fwo Cheng[2] is going to be different: The adorned palace will be within (merit and virtue) and what's outside will not obstruct the heart, or ears, or eyes – simple, natural, expansive, and peaceful. "You should be able to tell by now which places keep the precepts and which don't," said the Abbot after visiting the last temple. Purity and defilement leave trails, auras. We can feel it immediately – all the intuitive dials register.

Bio-feedback research verifies that we pick up and respond to subtle changes long before the discriminating mind alerts to them. In fact, these kinds of kinetic behaviors are more influential and basic than what we think of or intellectualize. Our control becomes lax without practice. Cultivation is learning to read ourselves, the world below the surface and behind the manifestations, and to reverse the flow of being pulled around by our noses (eyes, ears, tongue, body, and mind) in a suffering circle of birth and death.

---

2. The City of Ten Thousand Buddhas

The best bio-feedback equipment is just an extension of our own natural tools. Because we are so scattered and lazy, we have come to rely on machines. This is just an attachment. Because it is external, it threatens our independence. Whoever has the machine has the power to control and manipulate. The possibilities are very real, simple, and mind-boggling.

On the other hand, learning to "return the light and illumine within" is by far more natural and keeps things above board. Laziness on this level costs a lot in the end. A short-cut could easily turn you into a robot singing someone else's tune.

The fact that we don't know to return our light means that we are wide open to others stealing it. Either we control ourselves or we will be controlled. That which we fear or don't understand in ourselves is our Master.

Dharma seeds.

In flight on the way to Hong Kong from Bangkok a stewardess stared over Kuo Jing's shoulder, entranced for minutes. What is she staring at? The Avatamsaka Sutra, a few lines that Kuo Jing is translating. The stewardess moved her lips silently voicing the words and giving it a try herself. Worlds stop and hearts merge in inconceivable ways.

* * * * * * * * *

Hong Kong

September 17, 1978
Day 51 : Wonderful Dharma Monastery

The delegation arrived at the Kaitak Airport the day before at 8 p.m. The welcoming party include DM Hsi Ch'en, DM Chin Shan, Bhikshuni Ch'eng Ming and other dharma masters and disciples. They spent the night at Wonderful Dharma Monastery.

The Abbot to Dharma Master Hsi Ch'en's expansionist ambitions of a Buddhist empire with its headquarters based in New York:

"Why don't you just come over and join in our work at the City of Ten Thousand Buddhas? Isn't one center for World Buddhism enough? My interests are not regional. My perspective is great function for the entire substance. I don't care to carve out niches for myself in any part of the world. I'm not interested in making a name for myself. My sole concern is Buddhism and propagation of the Proper Dharma."

The Abbot offers some brief words over lunch:

"Dear Good Knowing Advisors, old and young friends, highly virtuous ones, today we're able to gather together in this new hall. This is due to conditions planted from measureless kalpas, and not at all a chance meeting. Yet, we will only truly meet in the Pure Land of Eternal Still Light, not in this Saha world of the five turbidities. Our enjoyments should not be limited to eating some good food together..."

The commotion at the Kaitak International

Airport, Hong Kong. September 1978.

A group portrait of the delegation at the

Kaitak International Airport, Hong Kong

歡

美國三藩市金山寺

宣 化 大

香港佛教聯合會會長覺光   香港

The Master and the delegation is received

迓
文　美國化界大學校長
法師莅港
伽聯合會會長洗塵暨四眾弟子恭迓

by the local sanghans and disciples

Heng Sure • September 17, 1978
It's first class – big, glossy and posh

Wonderful Dharma Temple.

Craftier, foxier, one cut above. Faster, smoother. Bigger. "Empty-handed you go see King Yama; all your tears are to no avail." Do you want your life's efforts to be set in stone and paint? Are you willing to cash in for the comfort and convenience of this skin bag? This place asks the question: "Do you cultivate mundane dharmas or transcendental Dharma?"

This new Bodhimanda is the finest of external forms. The biggest Buddha images Yang Tai Sheng could build. The finest modern frescoes in Asia, copied from the genuine originals. The most elegant guest rooms, baths, and restaurant that Hilton could build. On the surface it's first class. It's big and glossy, posh.

Where do the monks stay? Why is the restaurant in the center? Who asked for jet-set luxury in a Way-place? In the Buddha hall where do the people stand? If it hurts your neck to see the Buddha because he's so big, why not leave room for more people to see him? How many monks can you cram into the guest rooms? Where does the Sangha fit?

Hong Kong is too small, too ingrown. Decadent. The Abbot has come to the West, taught Americans, translated sutras, established the Five Schools, spread the Shurangama Mantra, the Great Compassion Mantra, transmitted precepts, taken forty left-home people – you won't find his name or his picture in the popular magazines. He does not own anything. He walks last. He does not seek advantages. He is not selfish. He works for others. As an ant, as a horse, as a road. When he says, "I am working for the Proper Dharma, for Buddhism," he can do so without blushing, without stumbling over his words, without shame.

This time in Malaysia, Singapore, Bangkok there has been a response. People have come by the thousands, stayed for three hours glued to their seats, taken refuge, learned a mantra for wisdom, two of the Forty-two Hands and Eyes, heard true principle, and gotten a boost of hope and light for the renaissance of the Proper Dharma at the City of Ten Thousand Buddhas.

Heng Chau • September 17, 1978
Hong Kong is not a playground

Impressions.

Business, politics in high density energy and competition – on the edge of a continent, the edge of demographic growth, the edge of the desire hype.

The pulse of Buddhism we felt in Malaysia, Singapore, and Bangkok was in the outer veins and arteries. Hong Kong and Taiwan are the heart and nerve centers.

Ah! The City of Ten Thousand Buddhas! Our teacher! The Plymouth and a long day of bowing. No money to buy a stamp, worn-out shoes, peaceful faces and clear eyes, one stick of incense, long Ch'an sits, the Avatamsaka Assembly, the laughter and excitement of Gold Wheel Temple, tattered robes and patched sashes, people too busy to sleep and always the unexpected and wonderful.

And yet, this is where the work is. This is where the Abbot goes – where no one else will go, where the Dharma is absent or threatened with extinction. This is the frontier. Armed only with vast vows and the four unlimited minds he knowingly dives into the hells in order to teach and transform the beings dwelling there.

There is a great humor (à la vonnegut) here that's easy to miss and end up in tears of despair.

The Abbot: "Hong Kong is not a playground. You have to be very careful here! Absolutely no scruples – they will do anything here, anything."

We visit a Buddhist hospital. With one glance, Kuo T'ung takes in the young nurses and decaying men lying half dead on hot beds. Connection?

The "high professions" of doctors and psychiatrists used to seem so ultimate and close to the secrets of life. But now those professionals just look like skinbag mechanics. The body is like a car – you cruise around in it for a spell, and it goes bad in degrees or disasters, but either way it goes bad. Who can hold on to it for long?

State.

Fire returning - waves of anger and irritation patiently ridden to calm and small understandings. Up and down, the mood swings between deep resolve and escape fantasies. Just a stage and a state – important not to pay attention to the short-term skirmishes and flack. Think big and broad, in measure of lifetimes.

Heng Sure • September 18, 1978
Day 52 : Western Bliss Garden

Buddhist Lecture Hall is a high-energy Bodhimanda – like a pearl that expands infinitely. Hong Kong island is like uptown Manhattan painted on an Asian backdrop. The air is hot and sticky. Hong Kong is so tight and jived – money.

When the tests came, I was half here, half leaking out. So when the chances to progress came, when the gates opened, I wasn't ready. Obstacles and conditions that I planted and made in the past kept me from connecting with the heart of it.

There's no one to blame – only a sigh. Patience and a brave grin and I start the merry-go-round once more. When the cause ground is true, the brass ring will naturally appear in your hand. Meanwhile, this time, I did not make it.

A regular mind-stopper, this ugly fishing village. We climbed four-hundred steps to Western Bliss Garden Temple, where the Master lived for years, surrounded by heavy poverty on the mountainside. Dirty shacks crammed and perched every which way, stacked on the contours of the slope like frail leaves piled below a cruel, bad-natured tree. When the heavy weather comes, or when drought or disease visits, it must be real hell.

> For all past bad karma...
> I now repent of it all.

Fighting a big battle with the sugar-drink desire. Nothing to do but bear it. No more Malaccas, no more testing that poison. I have no more question about me and sugar.

Seeking to make it all okay with the Abbot, he won't let me lean. He wants me to cultivate. Silence. Independence. Decisive strength. Since I missed my chance, at least I needn't make a mess when I splash.

Buddhist Lecture Hall.

It makes my heart ache to see the Hong Kong disciples. I thought we Americans were cold fish. These people are frozen past caring. The Abbot came full of light and good news for the future of the Proper Dharma in the West, and not one person asked to hear it. When he began to tell of Dharma successes he was ignored or interrupted. No one greeted him (but the three principle laywomen) – people popped in, bowed, and left. They treat him like a stranger. The old enemy Dharma Masters are now falsely buddy-buddy because of the City of Ten Thousand Buddhas and the Malaysian barnstorm.

Contrast.

The village around Western Bliss Garden is called "Town on the Horse's Back." It is like the other Hong Kong mountain slope shantytowns. Harsh weather stops life there. No clean water, no wood for fires or lights, electric wires down, disease spreads, pit toilets and sewers overflow. Drought is cruel, bringing suffering within suffering.

The delegation at Western Bliss

Garden, Hong Kong, September 1978

If it weren't for the television sets that fill the people's minds with false thoughts and desires, it could be the sixteenth century in Europe, or the London slums in Elizabethan times, or California during the Dusts Bowl migration. Suffering in poverty is timeless and international.

Below the Buddhist Lecture Hall is another horseback town: the Royal Hong Kong Jockey Club. More money and syndicate swank than most states in the Union. Gross waste, corrupt, decadent, sinful. We simple monks and nuns live in another world.

Heng Chau • September 18, 1978
Like lambs among a pack of wolves

We moved to the Abbot's Buddhist Lecture Hall in Hong Kong and bowed there in the afternoon while the Abbot put the heat on everyone for not cultivating, being phoney, and gossiping, etc.

The vibrations in this small hall on the eleventh floor, downtown, are clean and familiar. I felt at home as soon as the bus pulled to a stop. Old pictures of the Abbot, the pioneer days here and at Gold Mountain Monastery in San Francisco – sifting for gold nuggets, bitter work, lots of sacrifice and renunciation. What patience! We are constantly being scrutinized and tested with food, sweets, praise, ostracism, offerings. Nothing is what is seems.

The Abbot has taken a scolding, stern and hard nosed stance since arriving. Everyone has felt the sting of his teaching sword. Why? We are all getting lax and scattering here without knowing it. He's zapping our wits back into us. Here a casual mistake could bring disastrous results to our trip as well as to each person in the delegation. He's also teaching his Hong Kong disciples. This place is incredibly dangerous – end of the long mobile session. The danger here is extremely subtle and camouflaged. We are all like lambs in a pack of wolves and hunters disguised as our parents and benefactors.

Heng Sure and I often wonder what it would be like to just go and go until time and days and states all disappeared. Few of us take the chance to experience what we know is true: that there is no time, all our plans and ties are temporary and must end, that there's something beyond what we think is our limit.

Sometimes natural disasters, the death of one close to us, or a traumatic experience can jolt us out of our comfortable dream world. But we scramble back to "normal," dividing this and saving that until we are safely entangled in the mind web.

I know this is true, yet I still have the urge to get out of bowing and hang on to the mind web. My thoughts wander and drift to fantasies and nonsense in order to hold the illusion web together. When there's a clear space it only lasts a minute before I weave it back into the sticky web where there's no light. To a spider hanging on the ceiling it's we who are upside down.

We lost sight of the danger and our solidarity of purpose is scattering, so the Abbot is providing an alternative by his grabbing the center stage and doing everything he can to keep us single-minded and protected. All attention is focused on him. Some are afraid, others disgusted, some are trying to please, others hoping he'll leave. This is the "end" he warned us weeks ago to be careful about – where everything could be lost.

In fact, there is no end. There's only advance, and each step is steeper. This has been our experience on *san bu yi bai*. Who is willing to keep going on with the work? Who wants to escape and end the trip? Heng Sure and I are not the pick of the crop, as warriors go, but we know there's no relaxing – how much the less any form of retreating. Personal cultivation and the well-being of the Dharmarealm merge somewhere and become the same.

The Abbot finally accepted a bite of food to eat after forty-eight hours. He relaxed, wiped his brow and sighed,

"(Human) life is a big pain. It's false as we are born (falsely created) and it's false as we die (falsely destroyed). Sigh."

The crisis is past.

Leaving Home.

Leaving home is a big deal. We need to take it seriously. American left-home people, especially, don't want the responsibility (moral, spiritual, and social) that the vows and role hold. We prize our casual easy-come / easy-go attitude – sloppy about details and appearances, not respectful of rituals and rules. We make our own style and "to hell with 'em all," etc. But, this isn't an ordinary trip – there's level upon level of goings on here and it affects the entire welfare and peace of the Dharmarealm. It's our responsibility to come up to the sash and vows and it's not the case that the vows and sash should come down to suit us.

Feeling drained and wasted is the result of losing concentration and running out, even with thoughts. Today I ran out like a mother hen, fretting over people in the group, getting careless, and losing it. This is not my business or responsibility. A worried mind does no one any good. I gave up my bowing samadhi for a deviant samadhi and lost my power. "Be a man of the Way with no mind – mount the wind and drive the fog." Just cultivate and don't run out and be "General Manager" of anything or anybody. That's just the emperor again. Let things happen naturally, don't force it. When you start to worry and lose a cool, relaxed attitude that's a cue you're off the mark and messing in the garbage. "Be pure, peaceful, and happy."

Ending all attachments and false thoughts is what it's all about. Wherever the Abbot goes he "turns" states and conditions to this center and is not turned by them. I was affected by hiking through a Hong Kong slum in the hills yesterday – absorbed the *yin* and depressing vibrations. The Abbot, on the other hand (as at the leper hospital), shone even more brightly and talked *yang* Dharma of heroes and great strength.

In all situations, the Abbot is doing the highest *tai chi* and reversing all states, returning them to the source, both in words and behavior, by gesture and humor. For a few minutes, people are able to taste a little of the peace and happiness that comes from letting go of hang-ups and covered hearts. They love it, and come back for more. The more they want it, the more they learn and the lesson is always the same, "Don't follow me, follow yourself – return the light and look within."

My head is splitting from fire, especially the forehead and temples. Why? Lunch. The food is swimming in oil and MSG – all wok-fried. There's butter for the bread, and peanut-butter and jelly – both are incendiaries.

The alternative is to eat rice and fruit, but there's not enough fuel there to bow with. Or, make up for fuel deficit with drinks. But all the drinks are milk/sugar, sweet combinations that just bring desire thoughts.

The climatic heat of Southeast Asia, plus the food, has made it tough going – lots of *yin* battles with either not enough energy or too much desire. Rashes, diarrhea, headaches, and general lack of vigorous spirit hang over all of us. Except for the Abbot – he just keeps saying, "Everything's okay. No problem."

Heng Sure • September 19, 1978
Day 53 : Eastern Lotus Enlightenment Garden

Bowing at Eastern Lotus Enlightenment Garden. The finest Buddhahall of the trip. Tall, colored windows – golden light. Plain walls, simple, large graphics. Polished wooden floors, oval shapes, curved ends; stairs up to it from entryway far below. Tall roof, three stories, with balconies on all sides, windows on each level. Like Guggenheim. Huge red banners, hanging down two stories in front of the Buddha house. Ch'an benches are recessed into the walls – broad, flat cushions. Giant hanging lanterns.

Here is a blend of Western simplicity and Buddhist adornment. The bones are pretty (*feng shui*) – the oval shape, the elevated feeling, the chapel-pagoda openness, the simple, elegant materials. Constant movement from the banners, a tinkling from a wind chime, and yellow light from the third-story cupola windows, a huge bell and drum. Well planned and well done.

The Abbot: "You people are *kuai wu* (strange objects) – weirdos. Okay, be weird! Don't talk at all. People can be transformed by your silence, but as soon as you talk you become less interesting and become ordinary. Especially when there is the language problem, what you say for the most part is wasted, no meaning. The Dharma is alive, it's not dead.

"Just be sincere while you bow and let that do the talking for you. No need to explain anything, as you have to do on the road. This is a Buddhist place – they know what you're doing.

"All right you three, go out and transform all the Hong Kong types that I can't transform."

Heng Chau • September 19, 1978
When the mind and body are focused

"If you can't cut off desire, you can't transcend the mundane world," says the Shurangama Sutra. In fact, this is the heart of cultivation: transforming sexual desire into bright wisdom. With thoughts of desire comes seeking and with seeking comes all the trouble. I have learned to conceal and defer my desire, but the thought is there, and it's all the same.

Transforming desire ultimately is a question of wisdom. Nirvana, for example, has been defined as a state of "not produced, not destroyed," i.e., desire is not produced and wisdom is not destroyed. As soon as desire arises, wisdom vanishes and then we do upside-down things. Wisdom manifests naturally with concentration. When the mind and body are focused, the fire of desire comes under control and lights up the mind.

Heng Sure • September 20, 1978
Day 54 : Be careful with the affinities you create

> Here we are, and here we'll stay,
> For another seven days.
> Everyone is going under,
> Turned by Hong Kong's tarnished wonder.
>
> Falsely born, we falsely die;
> Life is empty, death's a lie.
> Dizzy from the sticky heat,
> Dipped in oil and drunk on sweets.
>
> Crushed in crowds and feeling faint,
> Western Paradise it ain't.
> Take me from this greedy town,
> Never felt so upside-down.
> Buddhadharma's brilliant light,
> Dim in Hong Kong's gloomy night.
>
> Takes a Bodhisattva's power,
> To cultivate from hour to hour.
> Vows and precepts must survive,
> To guide me through the dusty jive.

Be careful with the affinities you create. You might become a teacher of disciples in Hong Kong. What an unpleasant karmic job. This is where the Bodhisattva does his work. "Spare no blood or sweat, never rest."

The Abbot practices what he preaches. He is connected to us all by his vows. We have to become Buddhas first. What a hero he is. It makes me want to do nothing but try my best in every thought, every (silent) word – and in every move I make. No self. No greed. No falseness.

I'm beginning to fathom a bit of the teacher/disciple relationship. The teacher is a person who has skill and wisdom that the disciple wants also. The Buddhadharma requires a complete transformation of the deepest corners of the heart. Only with the teacher's help can the student be successful. Sometimes the student forgets what he is after. If the teacher is kind, he will remind the student and show him the road he needs to follow. On the way to success there are lots of potholes, traps and blind roads. It takes patient strength.

Heng Chau • September 20, 1978
Because they think it's bad luck

Hong Kong: cynical spiritualism; money worship. Monks are scorned and looked down upon, especially Western ones.

Kuo T'ung: "You know why everyone says 'Amitofwo' here when they see a shaved headed Sanghan?"

Heng Ch'au: "No, why?"

Kuo T'ung: "Because they think it's bad luck! They feel they might catch it and end up without any money, and so they say 'Amitofwo' to break the bad luck."

Heng Ch'au: "Really?"

Kuo T'ung: "Yeah. Even in the fancy office buildings – a well-dressed businessman saw us and spun around in his swivel chair and shouted, 'Oh Amitofwo.'"

Bow a lot, sit long, and shut up!

Each time the bowing gets sincere, I get sick. Today it's nausea, fatigue, and pounding headache. Since coming to Asia I've never been well and strong. It's been one thing after another. My heart is strong and clear, but my body won't cooperate. Rashes, diarrhea, infections, fever, etc., on and on. I must have some heavy karma here. The Abbot keeps saying, "Good, good, when Heng Sure tells him I'm sick. This skin bag is a bother!"

Free ride.

The only fat people in Asia are monks, bankers, and foreigners. One primary criteria of social change is going from hand to mouth to producing a surplus. As soon as there's a little extra, someone moves in on it and a new class develops that doesn't work for what's needed for survival. But, they live off the sweat of others. The time set free from subsistence scratching is supposedly used to contribute something special to the group and culture, traditionally creating artists, doctors (shamans), priests, and lately politicians, royalty, etc. Some contribute, and some just eat.

Buddhism is the highest expression of this most basic of needs. Monks and nuns should push to the limits in their Way cultivation so that others can follow and end suffering. "Fat" left-home people are cheats who climb on conditions. They take without transferring merit and virtue. In the end this is being unfilial, and children who don't treat their parents well live to regret it. There are no free rides in the Saha World.

Left-home people's special contribution is to go the ultimate – to get enlightened and realize our highest and most basic nature: Buddhahood. To carve a path and leave all greed, anger, and ignorance, and to perfect morality, samadhi, and wisdom. This is our work, and it's done for all, not for self. There is nothing more important or heroic than walking the Way!

Everything is impermanent and a dream – wealth, power, fame, and family. Not fearing suffering or being alone, we should burst through all obstacles, exhaust all doubts, tear apart the tigers of desire with our bare hands, and eat the fruit of the Way. Anything else is a cop-out and won't hold up under fire.

In most of Asia, Buddhism is for old ladies. Almost every temple has devout old people reciting sutras and sitting in corners fingering beads. Where are the young people? Young people go for the juice – the live current, the *yang*. They go where there's challenge, where there's growth and laughter and a bit of the real thing. They aren't in the temples. They aren't checking out the Buddhadharma in Asia.

Why? Because they go by what they can see and touch. Young people don't buy theories and tradition. They trust what they experience and follow what's in front of their eyes. When the Abbot came to Asia the young people got interested in Buddhism. The Buddhadharma is no more or less than what you are. The more you are for real, the more the Way manifests through you. The less real you are, the more people run away from you – even if you call yourself a Buddhist or an "Enlightened Master." The Dharma is not fixed or dead. It's just the teaching of all living beings.

September 22, 1978
Day 56 : You are not in tune with the times

In a evening lecture, Heng Sure explains why some Americans have so much faith in the Abbot:

"This is largely because the Abbot teaches with his own actions. During these sixteen years in America, he has endured what others cannot endure, eaten what others cannot eat, yielded what others cannot yield, done what others cannot do. Americans in general are extremely hard to tame and subdue; they are used to running around with so much freedom. Yet the Abbot persists with a mind that knows no loathing or weariness. With such awesome and boundless compassion, bit by bit he has moved his disciples to shame. Any other Dharma Master would have given up a long time ago. Americans are not particularly well-known for their filiality, but now many young people turn around and gratefully learn from the Dharma Master who has shown them the key to their true selves."

Afterwards, the Abbot speaks:

"In 1962 I left Hong Kong for America, and I've always felt apologetic towards the citizens of Hong Kong. I've never been able to truly benefit them, so even tonight as I speak to you I feel very ashamed.

"A long time ago I made a vow to translate all Buddhist sutras to other languages and widely propagate them, although I myself didn't know a single foreign language. This vow was not immediately realized, but I also made another vow, that I'll only allow the Proper Dharma to flourish wherever I go. I will not permit the coming of the Dharma-ending Age.

"Somebody is right now saying, 'You're mistaken. You are not in tune with the times. During the Dharma-ending Age, nobody cultivates, so no wonder nobody sympathizes with what you do.

"Although it is said to be the Dharma-ending Age, it all depends upon the people. If people cultivate, they can reverse the tide and make this the Proper Dharma Age. For it is said,

It is people that propagate the Dharma,
The Dharma does not propagate people.

If people hold precepts, give generously, practice in vigor, endure insults, cultivate concentration and wisdom, that itself is living out the Proper Dharma. There is no Proper Dharma Age or Dharma-ending Age, per se; people make it so. When people do not cultivate and nobody attains enlightenment, of course that is the Dharma-ending Age.

"In China I went everywhere to point out the need to translate the sutras, but I met with no support. Not until I came to America did I start getting a response. I went to America preparing to die there; that is why upon arrival I gave myself the name 'Monk in the Grave.' I've had many false names; none of them are real. Before leaving home my name was 'Living Dead Man,' which meant that I chose not to contend with anyone. In Manchuria after I left home I became known as An Tzu (Calming Compassion). In Hong Kong I used the name, Tu Lun (Saving Wheel). I also picked up a few more titles in Hong Kong that I wasn't counting on. I didn't know about them until I arrived in Malaysia this time. You might as well know about these names, if you do not already know them: I'm known as the Old Demon King, also as 'One of the Five Great Weirdos of Hong Kong.' I do not know who the other four weirdos are, but I kind of like this name. You see, I am a big weirdo, all my disciples are little weirdos, and we go around weirding people out. (Laughter; Chinese pun).

"Now, back to the subject under discussion: the translation of Buddhist sutras. It is a grand task. We began in 1968 and to date the International Institute of the Translation of Buddhist Texts has translated about thirty volumes of sutra texts. We will continue our efforts. We may make mistakes, but people who come after us can make the corrections. However, somebody has to start. In the past, the very few sutras that were available to Western readers were translated by Christian priests, ministers, or well-known scholars, but none had been translated from the inside. No left-home people who truly understood and at the same time cultivated the Buddhist principles had made translations. This was a great pity. The people who translate sutras in our institution in America don't do it for money; they feel it's a part of their duty to propagate the Dharma. None of the left-home people keep any private assets. All offerings go to the Central Funds of the Permanently Dwelling. We do not receive individual offerings.

"Now someone may wonder how we maintain a living. It comes through natural response with the Way. If you single-mindedly address yourself to the Way, other things will take care of themselves without your fussing over them. In order to combat the selfishness prevalent within Buddhism now, I have decided to give the City of Ten Thousand Buddhas to Buddhists of the entire world; not only to Buddhists, but to all people, all living beings. Someone must think I am really stupid, an old dolt who's lost his marbles. Yes, I've always been stupid like this. No matter how badly people treat me, I still treat them well; no matter how people scold or slander me, I still wish to benefit them.

"My disciples have learned to be stupid like me. Look at the two monks who are engaged in Three Steps One Bow. Their parents and former girlfriends write or call them, and they won't read the letters or answer the phone calls. Why? Because they have brought forth the mind to do something truly meaningful for all living beings. They have decided to give up their small selves for the big. Now, Heng Sure has taken a vow of silence, but he must have felt special affinities with you to have said so much tonight. For a mute to talk so much is inconceivable."

Heng Sure • September 22, 1978
Most of all, he needs a lieutenant

I'm innocent and naive, seeing purity in the mud. In this little flat, all the troubles of the world appear. The human mind is an affliction factory.

When you open wisdom you will be able to protect your teacher. He needs a lieutenant most of all. For him to have to hassle small details is too shameful. Taxis, planes, schedules, seeing and screening people, hassling food and drink – all this should be done by his helpers. None of us can do it right yet.

The Abbot should move in quiet, spaces, he should have total privacy when he wants it and access to people when he wants that. He should be protected. His work is huge, awesome, and it takes energy and time. We all look to him for our every need. It is really too much. It is killing him, and he will never complain.

He began in America by cooking for his disciples, teaching them how to play the instruments, how to speak Chinese, how to meditate, cultivate, eat, walk, and sleep. This is all at home. When we go out on tour, the problems multiply and we all go back to the kindergarten stage. We have not progressed very far from the start. Still passing the work to the Abbot – standing in his light. My part of the bargain is to cultivate and be quiet. It's hard, but anything less than my best is pure cheating.

Bowing: cleaning out inside.

Sometimes images appear and I know they are important. They burst like all the other thoughts; they dissolve and scatter like all conditioned dharmas, but there is a difference. These thoughts feel like king-pins, like seed cores, like roots. When these thoughts appear and vanish, cut back by the wisdom sword, they take a lot of darkness with them. Many tangles of ignorance are cut loose at the same time.

Today while meditating an important image arose. It was the instant when ignorance turns to sexual activity and the twelve links of causation begin. It is an instant of commitment. Man and woman look at each other and yield to the urge and the heat of sexual union. Before this moment there is still an option, a chance to hold on to purity and independent wisdom. Once action is conditioned by the sticky, dark, powerful momentum of ignorance it takes great strength of vows and will to keep the wheel from turning.

I saw the critical chance, remembered the moment, how it felt like putting the second foot onto the top of a long, slippery slide down to darkness. It felt like surrender to an ageless, unknown force. Bigger than individuals, full of humorless laughter and cruel, sad wisdom. It felt like walking into the mouth of an enemy immortal, a creature with an infinite appetite for light and life. This power existed to devour the light of goodness and to extinguish life. In return it gave a quick, thrilling spin on a turning wheel. Those who took the ride held on for a time and then lost their grip and spun off into one of six roads. The roads were circular as well, all leading back to the wheel, and the spinning, sliding, and returning went on and on.

Face to face with the urge, full of the heat, I took charge of my mind and swung the sword with all my strength. I wanted to totally clean away this thought for good – wanted to wipe this image off my taped memory bank.

I called on Guan Shi Yin Bodhisattva and recited my vows to end all sexual desire. Something inside broke and dropped away. I felt lighter and cleaner.

The next image was a woman, any woman, facing me from a distance. She was cool and disinterested. I could face her squarely without fear and without shielding. Nothing passed between us; no energy was lost in self-defense. Simple. This is how it should have been all along. But after I learned about men and women it got confused and dirty.

Heng Chau • September 22, 1978
The crowded dirty sidewalks are Alpine trails

Eating still hasn't balanced out. Before Malacca I could easily get by on one Middle Way meal a day. Since the sickness, however, when I run out of fuel there's nothing left to draw on, so weakness and false thoughts of food click in. The one meal then becomes too important. I tend to overeat in anticipation of running out of gas later in the day. But overeating doesn't solve that problem and only leaves me feeling stuffed and overfired.

The alternative is patience – sickness was one extreme and can't be corrected overnight with "over health," i.e., stuffing up on good food and vigorous exercise. It's going to take a while, but patience and more patience is the only method to rely on.

"Eating" a liquid breakfast is an expedient but requires a sharp eye on the Kid Greed and his gang. It's got to be bland and fuel only.

I've cut out butter, peanut butter, jelly until the natural fire returns. Artificial fire, including ginseng, has never suited me – it's a crutch and scrambles the natural mind/body harmony. As a short-term lift after a small loss it's tolerable, but for major imbalance it's a dangerous practice and can make things worse. Quick recovery and fast relief is just another kind of greed. It's easy to be healthy. Being sick should be the same: part of the Skin Bag Blues. Suffering and ecstasy are both unnatural extremes. They are empty and impermanent. First they appear and then they are gone. Relax and don't go with them.

> Retired deep in the mountains,
> Dwelling in a still place,
> Secluded far on a lonely cliff beneath the tall pines,
> I stroll and sit in quietness,
>   a monk at home in the wilderness,
> Filled with stillness and peace,
>   living in true light-heartedness

Dharma Master Yung Chia
Song of Enlightenment

Next to cultivating under the Master, packing alone in the mountains is where my heart sets straight. The same kind of states come up at a Ch'an session that I experience hiking the high country. What is false and empty is seen as false and empty. What is true and real can't be expressed or held. Everything is just as it is. The self-nature is not at all difficult to discover.

In Hong Kong I often pretend we are all cultivating in the mountains. The crowded dirty sidewalks are Alpine trails. The traffic rush is just the deep valley breezes, and the troubled, nervous faces of people I see as one who meets a stranger on the trail after a long time alone. I want to say "Shh, shh, it's okay."

September 23, 1978
Day 57 : At least you come out first in something!

In an evening talk, Dharma Master Heng Hs'ien speaks first. The title of her talk is, "The Stupid Ph.D."

"When I was a layperson I had managed to convince myself that I was pretty smart. Most people assume that Ph.D.'s have something up their sleeves, and so do the Ph.D.'s themselves. Only after I encountered the Buddhadharma did I realize that most scholars just like to think themselves intelligent. Chuang-tzu said that the thing dearest to many scholars is a good name. This craving comes from a bloated sense of self; their ego is too large. Only after meeting with a bright-eyed Good Knowing Advisor who could see right through my every flaw, who allowed me nowhere to hide behind my self importance, did I find out something about myself.

"The Abbot is always chiding me about two vile aspects within the American education system: one is the open book test, the other the cheating sheet. I never used to understand why he kept on harping on those two things. After all, I never cheated except occasionally when I was very young, and only out of mischief – this is how I used to rationalize. And it is only recently that I've begun to understand what the Abbot is talking about.

"You see, I've always had a cheating sheet inside my own mind. Like tonight, knowing that I am supposed to talk to you, I started calculating what to say, what pleasant things I can talk about to make it all sound good. And, as usual, I didn't have time to prepare beforehand. I've always relied on something outside of myself in everything I do, looking for crutches or props, adding a head upon a head, not returning to my own wisdom, but searching away from the source. That is the cheating sheet and the open book that my teacher has been talking about all these years. You've got to do the work yourself. There is no short cut and no easy way out.

"For example, if one really wants to study Buddhism, all one needs to do is to take refuge in the Triple Jewel, find a truly virtuous Good Knowing Advisor, and simply practice. But I went at it in a roundabout way. I went to the universities, trying to learn Buddhism from professors and books. Some time later I discovered that most professors do not know anything about real Buddhism, and that books are insufficient guidelines. The Buddhism that Shakyamuni Buddha taught concerns the truth within the Mind. It was brought by the Patriarchs from India to China, and later to the West, in a direct lineage that protects the secret of the Mind-Pulse, the Proper Dharma Eye treasury, transmitted only through the Mind sealing the Mind, and not through externals." (applause)

The Abbot then addresses the audience:

> "Purity is true blessings and nobody enjoys it;
> Afflictions are offenses and people grab them up.
> Name and fame are small matters
>   and all are fond of them;
> Birth and death are matters of great importance,
>   and no one pays any attention to it.

"If we get rid of greed, anger and stupidity, quite naturally our precept power, concentration, and wisdom will surface. Greed means having bottomless craving – left-home people saying that they don't want money but actually thinking the more the better – like myself. If Sanghans who are 'models of gods and men' behave like this, how much the more will laypeople? Because of endless greed the world becomes more and more corrupt every day.

"Once there is greed, there is selfishness. Why are you afflicted? Because you are selfish. You feel that people aren't being good to you, and you blow up in anger. If you're always mindful of others' benefits and forget yourself, how can you possibly become afflicted? That's why we recite:

> The evil karma I've committed in the past,
> Stems from beginningless
>   greed, anger, and stupidity,
> Which arise from my body, speech and mind.
> Of all this I now reform and repent.

"You should realize that 'Karmic offenses are basically empty, but if you haven't finished with them, you must pay up old debts.' It's only because our offenses are formless that we don't see them. If they had a shape or form, they would fill up the entirety of empty space. And, although they do not have any visible form or shape, they are nonetheless carried within our eighth consciousness-field, and so the verse says,

Even after hundreds and thousands of kalpas,
The karma you've created is not forgotten,
When the proper conditions combine,
You'll still have to undergo the retribution.

"Last night I said to you that I feel apologetic towards my friends in Hong Kong. This wasn't uttered casually. I really mean it. I lived in Hong Kong from 1949 to 1962, with half a year spent in Thailand and one year in Australia. Every day I tried to propagate the Dharma, but this is a very peculiar place. If you speak the truth, nobody believes you; if you tell them falsehoods, people are happy to accept them. I've always adhered to the principle that 'The straightforward mind is the Bodhimanda,' but it didn't quite seem to work here. However, even if people do not believe it, I still have to say what I have to say."

The Abbot then launches into a light-hearted account of the typhoon story and the water shortage in Hong Kong:

"Once there was a great water shortage in the colony, and all the temples in Hong Kong started praying for rain, but to no avail. After several months, as things were getting really bad, I said to one of my disciples, 'Liu Kuo Chuen, you recite the Buddha's name every day, now I want you to do some hard reciting. If it doesn't rain within three days, you might as well never come up to Western Bliss Gardens again.' She was probably a little frightened, and she fervently recited day and night without stopping. After two and a half days the heavens opened and poured down buckets full. The problem of water shortage was completely solved. The next day the newspapers were full of it. Each temple claimed that it was their merit. All I could do was laugh. If it makes people happy, so be it.

"Now I am telling you these stories, not because I'm boasting or trying to make you bring forth faith in me. I'm just illustrating how with genuine sincerity there is always a response. I never told anyone about these incidents when I was living in Hong Kong, and I haven't broadcast them in America either, but now I see the time is right, so I can share a story or two with you.

"I'll also tell you a little bit of the Buddhism practiced in America. This teacher is a very stupid teacher, and Americans who have left home under him are also stupid. Otherwise why would they not desire any comfort for themselves, like these two monks who just continue to bow without stop? These two people also made the vow not to handle any money. Heng Sure knows that money is dirty and doesn't want anything to do with it. Kuo T'ung used to like it too much; now he's resolved to kick the habit.

"To top it all off, I also have a stupid Ph.D. as a disciple. Tonight is the first time I heard her admit publicly that she's a stupid Ph.D. That probably makes her the first 'Stupid Ph.D.' in America, or even the first in the world. That's not bad! At least you come out first in something!

"When you've reached the ultimate level of stupidity and not-knowing, you can become truly wise. There is still hope for her. Her future is not dark."

Heng Sure • September 23, 1978
What he does is not very popular here

The Abbot has publicly praised us twice in Hong Kong for not reading or writing letters to our family and friends. One monk who had just left seclusion got a hard scolding for sending letters out during his seclusion. *San bu yi bai* was used as the example of how to do it right. "They don't read anything, not even letters from their parents and siblings. How about that?" said the Abbot.

One bite of mooncake: liver jumped, eyes blipped, pain in arms as veins dilated, lost my balance, heat changed, lost my sword, my mind's eye closed. Eyes drooped, shoulders hunched, spine wilted. You know what? You can't handle sugar. It trashes your body and mind.

Heng Ch'au: "What the Abbot does is not very popular here."

The Abbot: "No one understands what I do, no one likes what I do. They say 'You are out of step with the times – a throwback.' I propagate the Proper Dharma during the Dharma-ending Age, because I feel that if there are no sages around then the Dharma has come to an end. And if you don't cultivate, there won't be any sages."

(To a laywoman) "At no time can you be arrogant or self-satisfied. How can you feel you are special? Inside you stink all the same. You may not put on airs or be proud and haughty. To decorate yourself with finery this way is just adorning a toilet, right? What's the difference? Inside you stink."

Heng Chau • September 23, 1978
Today I feel clear, strong, and happy

Bowing at Eastern Lotus Enlightenment Gardens – a special place, full of light and the "clear and empty room" inside and outside.

Today I feel clear, strong, and happy – like a child again with the "morning *chi*." Somewhere today while bowing I felt the burden and *yin* cloud of this old sickness lift off my mind. Everything became sunny and lighthearted. Like Kuo T'ung said after lunch, "I don't know why, but suddenly I lost my taste for mooncakes. Even peanut butter and jelly went down hard." So it was with my taste for girls.

All day, while bowing under the old painting of smiling sages sitting alone in the mountains and by streams, I felt my true spirit returning to a place before I knew sex. It was like being let out of prison: I kept smiling and felt I shared a secret with the "weirdo" cultivators in the paintings.

September 24, 1978
Day 58 : I've been an ant, a mosquito, a dung beetle

The Abbot's address tonight:

"When the nature is still and demons subdued,
　　there is happiness every day.
When false thoughts do not aries,
　　there is peace everywhere.

When the mind ceases and thoughts stop,
　　there is true nobility and wealth.
When private desires are completely severed,
　　there is a true field of blessings.

"Everything begins and ends with the mind. Confucius says of the heart,

If you restrain it, it comes under control;
If you let it go, it runs berserk.
Coming and going, it is not fixed as to time;
You cannot fathom its direction.

"To cultivate the Mind Ground simply means to recognize that we reap what we sow – every bit of it. Why have some of us cultivated so long and still not opened enlightenment or attained the fruition? It's because the karma we create is a mixture of good and evil. Confused, we do not slice through situations and recognize them as they truly are. We do good things that are mixed with the bad and bad things that are mixed with the good. We are not clean. Because we flow with the ordinary person's current of the six dusts, and turn our backs on the enlightenment of the sages, we do not attain enlightenment. We allow ourselves to be borne along by the tumultuous currents of the eyes, ears, nose, tongue, body, and mind

– the six defiling organs – and become embroiled in ceaseless revolving among the six dusts. The eye sees form-dust and latches onto form; the ear hears sound-dust and runs after sound; the nose smells the dust of odors and becomes turned by smell; the tongue tastes the dust of flavor and craves taste; the body feels the dust of contact and becomes confused by sensations; the mind grabs on to dharmas and becomes conditioned by dharmas. We behave like yoked cattle, pulled hither and thither without any control over our destinies. The Avatamsaka Sutra says,

> If one wishes to completely understand
> All Buddhas of the three periods of time,
> One should contemplate the nature
>   of the Dharma Realm:
> Everything's made from the mind alone.

"Your mind is the host, the master-control; it should not be turned by states. If you become happy when a little benefit befalls you, or disgruntled as soon as something unpleasant happens, you're just being turned by states. People who cultivate should always think of the well-being of others. Do not cultivate only for yourselves; give your entire body, mind, nature, and life to the world.

"Why are we selfish or jealous? Because we have a self. Once you have a self, an ego, you'll envy others who are better or more talented than you. With jealousy you're in big trouble; this is a sure way to end up in the hells.

> A single thought of hatred arises,
> A million doors of obstruction open up.

"By entertaining one bit of jealousy or resentment, you can fall into the spaceless hells. After measureless kalpas of suffering you will be reborn as hungry ghosts. Having paid up your dues, you'll gain rebirth in the path of animals. As what animals? As bugs, as dung beetles. You'll be stuck in the outhouse, trapped in that horrible stench for countless aeons, feeding on excrement and drinking urine – such is the retribution for being jealous. Or, if you're really selfish you'll become a mosquito. Mosquitoes drink other people's blood to satisfy their own hunger; they harm others in order to sustain themselves. This is just a carry-over from a habit of gross selfishness and self-seeking in their previous lives.

"Somebody is wondering: 'Dharma Master, how do you know about all these states? Do you read about them from the sutras?' I know about them because I've experienced all of them in my past lives: I've been an ant, a mosquito, a dung beetle... I've planted such causes and reaped such effects. Therefore, what I tell you is absolutely true. There is not a single trace of falsehood or idle speculation about it. If you do not believe me, you may try it out for yourselves, but it may be too late by the time you find out.

"Most living beings rotate within the Wheel of the Six Paths and never escape. We've forgotten our true homes, and are content to drift from one motel to another. So we wander aimlessly through lifetime after lifetime, suddenly we're in the heavens, suddenly in the hells, suddenly a god, suddenly an asura, suddenly a human, suddenly a ghost or an animal – don't you think this is a great pity?

"You should recognize clearly that life is but a dream. Now, most people do not like to hear this. If you were dreaming and someone came up to you and told you, 'Hey, you're just having a dream,' you probably wouldn't believe them. After you awakened you'd know, even if people didn't tell you. The same situation applies to our lives now. Before you're enlightened, you won't believe that this existence is just a dream; after you've opened enlightenment, you'll know without anyone telling you."

Heng Sure • September 24, 1978
I got turned by this place in two days

The grease and clamor of Hoeh Ming Temple in Kuala Lumpur
was not a lot different from the sedate canopied plaza of the genteel
Singapore Buddhist Lodge to us who bow *san bu yi bai*. The marble
floor and the roaring fans in the Bangkok Chinese Buddhist Association's Buddhahall felt the same as the polished hardwood and
stained glass hush of Hong Kong's Tung Lien Chia Yuan chapel.

The California highway is not the same until the mind that bows
to the Buddhas is the same. At that time the Dharmarealm returns to
one piece and the mind is quiet. Outside is made from inside.
Outside reflects inside.

"When the Nature's in samadhi, the demons are quelled
and every day is happy. When false thoughts no longer arise,
then every place is peaceful."

This state of bliss can come from your mind. How many miles
away is your present state of pain?

Heng Sure: Shih Fu, your greatness came home to me today.
How anyone but a Bodhisattva could live in this toilet for ten years
and not turn and not fall – it's your vow-power and your solid Way-
mind that moves me. I got turned by this place in two days.

September 25, 1978
Day 59 : The three types of Buddhism

Heng Sure delivers a talk in the evening about Buddhism:

"There are three types of Buddhism in the world: the Buddhism
of Greed, the Buddhism of Anger, and the Buddhism of Stupidity.

"The first kind, the Buddhism of Greed, can be called Marketplace Buddhism. Everything can be bought and sold here; it is run

like a business. Temples become excuses for big hotels, restaurants, or amusement parks for tourists. Monks operate them like businessmen. The Dharma-door of hustling Dharma protectors is cultivated here.

"The second kind is the Buddhism of Anger. Here obstructiveness and jealousy are the main characteristics. People vie with one another to put up the best appearance, fighting to see who builds the tallest statue, the largest temple, the most ornate images, or the best vegetarian restaurant in town. Dharma Masters compete with each other for disciples, pitting Dharma-protectors against one another. Some Dharma Masters set themselves up as emperors, with their own retinues and armies. They look down on people who are not as strong as they and envy those who are more capable.

"The third type is the Buddhism of Stupidity, also called the Buddhism of taking a loss. The adherents are not as bright as the previous two schools. They don't know how to maneuver business deals, or seek advantages from conditions or fight with each other. They are willing to walk behind everybody else, willing to take on suffering, to follow the rules, and comply with the truth – that's why they are called stupid.

"This type of Buddhism is not very popular these days, yet all of you should consider: what is really stupid, what is truly wise? If Shakyamuni Buddha were alive, which type of Buddhism do you think he would support? It's said that the greatly wise appear like fools, and the truly eloquent speak clumsily. If you possess true wisdom, you needn't put on a false front and try to impress people with your cleverness. Now, all of you know where this brand of Buddhism is taught. If you agree that we have some use for it, then you should attend the School of the Buddhism of Stupidity, work to propagate the Proper Dharma, and graduate from that school."

The Abbot then speaks:

"Upon coming to Asia, this delegation is having a lesson in the Buddhadharma at all moments of the day. This stupid teacher learns from his stupid disciples, and the stupid disciples learn from the stupid teacher. We learn stupidity from each other until we've mastered the art of being stupid. Then we'll slowly turn it around to wisdom. If you haven't learned how to be really stupid, it's not known whether you can learn to be truly wise. To get up to the top of the mountain you have to start from the bottom. To build skyscrapers you build a foundation from the ground. So in every act, start from the very basis.

"In America, the learning situation is the same. All the students and faculty at Dharma Realm Buddhist University are learning the Buddhadharma every day, however much they can absorb. The Buddhism we study is not Indian, Chinese, Thai, Burmese, Ceylonese, Japanese, or Korean Buddhism; it is simply, Buddhism. Buddhism has no boundaries, no race, no sect. Shakyamuni Buddha has said, 'All living beings have the Buddha Nature. All can become Buddhas.' This truth does not apply only to living beings of some countries and not to others. Living beings fill up the entirety of empty space. That is why I've taken the liberty to call Buddhism the 'Teaching of Living Beings.' Every living being can become a Buddha, and all Buddhas can turn their wisdom and compassion boat around, transform into thousands and millions of living beings, and cultivate along with the sentient multitudes. In this way, the Buddhas and Bodhisattvas influence all beings to resolve their hearts on Bodhi.

"Amongst living beings, a human being is the one imbued with the highest potential for spiritual development. Hence, Buddhism is also called the 'Teaching of People.' It is people who become Buddhas. Now, all people have minds, so Buddhism is also the 'Teaching of the Mind.' Therefore, it is said, 'The Buddha, the mind, and living beings – the three are one and the same.' Since Buddhism has no nationality, no racial or cultural barriers, why do Buddhists willingly drive themselves into a small corner? Your heart's measure becomes smaller than that of a dustmote, and you become selfish and self-seeking. Now, ultimately, who's like this? Just me, I'm not talking about others. I am a deep offender within Buddhism, a rebel. But I wish to change towards the good and get rid of my selfishness. It's not that Buddhism is imperfect; it's that I haven't perfected my own self. It's not that other people are evil, but that I haven't succeeded in teaching and transforming them. That is why I always say,

> Truly recognize your own faults,
> Do not discuss the faults of others,
> Other's faults are just my own.
> Identity in substance is called
> Great Compassion.

I'm not afraid of evil people. The more evil they are, the more I want to move them towards the good, not only through pretty words, but through actual practice. We should become models, so that others can see for themselves. If you point out a certain road for people to go on, you should first have gone down that road yourself so that people will not stumble into peril.

"Now we have great affinities in order to meet like this. We should help each other. What I say may not be correct, but all of you should use your own wisdom to judge what is correct or not. I tell my disciples in America not to blindly believe in me; they should employ their own wisdom. If you cultivate your wisdom, you will eventually obtain the Dharma Selecting Eye. Don't wear shoes on your head, or put on a hat for your shoes.

"Now, ultimately, what is right and what is wrong? Basically there is nothing which is absolutely right or wrong. Something which you regard as right, when viewed from another angle may become wrong, and vice versa. Hence,

> The Way is to tread on one side
> But principle is discussed on both ends.

So, as to whether things are correct or not, don't ask others, just use your own Vajra Jeweled Sword and very honestly recognize your own faults. For example, for those of us who cultivate, do we have any greed? You can test yourself out very easily. Left-home people can ask themselves: 'Do I strike up false thoughts about Dharma-protectors all day long?' If you do then you're not beyond greed; if you do not it means that you have less greed, but not that it has completely vanished. When you encounter a state, say someone gives you a red envelope, do you start calculating: is there one dollar, or ten, or a hundred, or a thousand dollars inside? If you toy with such questions within your mind you still have greed. If you don't it means you have temporarily squelched your greed mind – that's all – not that it has left for good.

"When delicious things appear on the table, do you want to eat more than your normal share? This is a very good test. Do you desire savory foods, do you recite the Sutra of Food and Drink for everyone? This is a sutra you recite to the laypeople, saying, 'Yesterday so and so prepared a scrumptious meal for me, they used the best of ingredients, and I ate a double portion.'

"When you see others wearing pretty clothes, do you start wishing for clothes like theirs? When you see others living in comfortable houses do you start wishing for a palatial mansion? In everyday mundane affairs – eating, wearing clothes, sleeping – you can understand your own greed. Don't cheat yourself. If you have greed, then change it; if you don't, then proceed with what is proper. The worst thing to do is fritter your time away. This is the most painful thing of all.

"Now I have come from America, which is a most democratic country. Every time I finish lecturing the sutras or speaking the Dharma I always ask people for feedback or criticism. Hence, I welcome whatever questions you may have."

Someone asks: "Since the Venerable Dharma Master had been able to control the typhoons for over ten years when he was living in Hong Kong, will he be so compassionate as to stop all typhoons from coming to Hong Kong altogether?"

The Abbot laughs and answers, "You might as well ask me to stop all the people in Hong Kong from dying altogether." (loud laughter and applause) "What you requested is not possible. In anything I can help people with – if I have to wait to be asked – then it's too late!"

***

Heng Sure • September 25, 1978
In Hong Kong, it is instant replay

Tough state. Feels like my insides are made of boiling sand – harsh, bitter. The body's full of lobster claws. It's a Scorpio feeling. It's called thwarted desire. There's an urge to release it any way possible, but sex is not an option. Those tubes don't connect any longer. Fighting is not it – I don't want to pound and beat. The weakest urge is to dilute the inner lava with sweet drinks, or find someone to talk with, or go sightseeing. Come lunchtime it's going to be hard to keep the lid on it. Food is the big one for me now, and even so it's not very big. One wrong bite can blow it.

When I bow and sit in Ch'an this lava turns to good juice. It circulates, like it should. Then the pressure lifts in the right way for cultivation. But, once the pressure goes, so does the caution and the governor that keeps the desire in. That's the time not to let it go flowing out.

"Why are you still on the wheel? Because last life although you made real progress, in this life you retreated. Back and forth like this forever. You've turned and spun on the wheel. You've got to maintain a solid thought for cultivation. Be constantly true." (the Abbot)

So as it was in life after life, so it is in minute after minute. Smelt a batch, then be patient. Don't change. Don't blow up your furnace while you gather more material. Be smart. Control yourself.

Come to think of it, Hong Kong is a special school. A place to learn about the original face of human beings. We learn firsthand, as all the worst parts of greed, anger, and stupidity rise up inside. In

America and Canada everything is new and fresh and open. There is always more space to explore. Dirty habits don't return for immediate feedback. Hong Kong is instant replay with all the ugliness intact.

Letting the emotion go for the time being, take another look at Hong Kong. More than anywhere, Fragrant Harbor is the world's marketplace. The morals and the methods of the market fill the air and cover the ground. Everything is bought and sold, including religious practice. There is nothing holy, nothing pure. It all has a price. How can one survive as a cultivator of pure practices in Hong Kong?

The Abbot: "This place is special. If you tell someone the truth, they will not believe you. If you tell a lie, you will find believers – that's Hong Kong."

I have the image of a log-rolling race. Everyone must move faster and faster to stay upright. Or it's a vibrating trampoline. All the people dance madly like puppets just to stay up and in place. Once you go down you can't get back up, it's moving too fast. The world needs a Hong Kong. Every house needs a toilet.

Hong Kong is a classroom. We come to learn about the worst in all of us. Our teacher taught here for ten years. What vow-power. He was not turned by it.

Yessiree Bob, I've got the Hong Kong flu. I've got to get smarter. It's time to stop being stupid. It's time to recognize myself and protect the valuable part. How?

When it's proper Dharma, give myself to it one hundred percent. When it's any other thing, hold it all back one hundred percent. When it's my practice and my teacher, stop holding back. When it's for others, give it all. When it's leaking out for sense pleasures and turning in the dust, slam the door and say, "No!" Don't be stupid and sloppy. The world is too dirty, too harsh, the outward face of living beings is too ugly for me to waste my chance to cultivate out of it.

Serve wisdom, starve ignorance, take the light, give away the darkness, protect the good – the true; trash the evil – the false. I've got the Hong Kong flu. It's time to get smarter.

Into the red alert — it feels like the last phase of a military evacuation. Under full armor we will depart from the marketplace — dragging our trophies, dangling the last-minute gifts, shouldering our sleeping comrades, guarding our jewels.

Last time, from Kuala Lumpur, I lost big because I didn't watch myself. I got into a phoney super-dramatic hype and like any other attachment, it pulled me off center and scattered my concentration.

What was true in Big Sur is true in Hong Kong. It has been my teaching these ten days: if you let anything, any state, move you away from your work in turning the wheel, then you are turned by the state. All states arise from within. If you stop or dwell for any reason, good or bad, pleasant or unpleasant, big or small, then you have been fooled. This is basic. Turn your wheel all the time. All dharmas are uniform, level and equal. Don't pick and choose among them and come out seeking and chasing.

How many times will you make this mistake? The Abbot must feel like a tape recorder — he's said it so often and in so many ways.

"The free man of the Way has connected with the Tao. He is not bound up by the dust. He is not like all beings who from beginningless time in the past until today have turned their backs on enlightenment and united with the dust. And in thought after thought, amidst all the illusory states, they follow along with all kinds of dust. At no time do they stop, how much the less do they escape from them.

"One who studies the Tao can turn ten thousand things and is not turned by them. His eyes see a thousand different things and his mind relaxes them into a single state. Under the trees or beside the stream he nurtures the sage's womb. He sees the moon's beauty and he roams at ease. He hears the bubbling spring and he is *dz dzai.*"

Song of Enlightenment
Dharma Master Yung Chia

September 26, 1978
Day 60 : Last day in Asia

On the last day of lectures, the Abbot speaks:

"All of you Good Knowing Advisors, this is the last of the five days of our lecture session. I know that during the past few days some people have been entertaining false thoughts, violently opposing what I have said. But tonight the battle is over, and I honestly hope that I am the loser, that all of you with false thoughts in your heads turn out to be the ultimate winners. However, we Buddhists should be frank and out-in-the-open, so you shouldn't hide under a false front. No matter how you feel about me, whatever it is that you do not like, you're welcome to bring out in the open, so that we can all discuss and learn from it. Whatever is in accord with the Way, progress with it; if not, then retreat from it. Do not wrangle inside yourself.

"Now why are there wars in the world? Just because there are wars inside everybody's minds. Inside your mind you are always fighting – it has become a battlefield.

> Contention creates an attitude of winning or losing.
> It is an opposition to the Way.
> Once the mind of the Four Marks appears,
> How can one attain Samadhi?

"Cultivating the Way means not contending. Ultimately, there is no principle worth arguing about. Once you start comparing or arguing, you fall from the Path. You've brought forth the mark of self, the mark of others, the mark of living beings, and the mark of a life-span. How can you attain proper concentration and proper reception this way?

"Take a look. Why do people's hair turn white? Because they have too many false thoughts. There's too much war going on inside themselves, and they exhaust their gasoline supply. If you remember me from my days in Hong Kong, I used to have fairly white hair the years right before I left. When I arrived in America I took one look at the mirror and said to myself, 'My gosh, what have you done?' I realized I had been doing too much false thinking, so I decided to give up the habit altogether. And my hair turned black again. Confucius said,

> Before happiness, anger, sorrow, or joy arise, there is the Middle Way. If these emotions are brought forth in the opportune time, then one attains Harmony.

With regard to the emotions of life, you should watch over them and not let them control you. If you indulge in any of them you will not thrive in peace and prosperity; instead darkness and bad luck will take over.

"Before, when I was living in Hong Kong, I had a penchant for reprimanding people. I thought, 'The straightforward mind is the Way Place,' and felt fully justified in voicing my complaints. Yet I found out that it didn't work. All I succeeded in doing was to convince people that Dharma Master Tu Lun was a glaring-eyed Vajra, so ferocious! So, upon arriving in America I changed and reformed my ways. I started bowing to my disciples. Whenever my disciples make mistakes, I bow to them a few times… Have you ever seen a teacher like this?

"This is because I believe that 'The disciple always excels the Master.' I am willing to walk underneath the feet of all my disciples, serving as a road for them, and will certainly not tread on top of their heads. And although some disciples are still a little afraid of me, most of them know that I am just a paper tiger. Now, on this Asian tour, I've brought with me three Ph.D.s, and three people with Master's degrees. I am an illiterate myself. I know nothing. In America I've been lecturing the Avatamsaka Sutra the past seven years, and when one of my old buddies in Hong Kong heard of this he exclaimed,

'What, him lecturing the sutras? But he hardly knows how to read!' You can see from this that I'm really one of no knowledge. Now, having gone to America the situation is even more intensified. In China I could at least pull off a few characters, but I'm completely at sea with the ABC's (laughter). And if someone like me who can't read is lecturing the sutras, how much more should people who know how to read lecture sutras? How can they be lazy?

"So in America, I'm lecturing day and night, up and down, right and left, and they don't really understand what I am saying. I can pull the wool over my students' eyes because they do not understand Chinese. Now I've brought with me a group of American disciples who can pull the wool over your eyes, since a lot of you do not understand English. So you see, this Dharma Master is a big quack. If you want to be taken for a ride, you're welcome to listen along. If you don't, well then just plug up your ears. I'll tell you some more unbelievable things to cheat you with.

"Before we came over to Malaysia we knew the weather would be very hot, and I told the members of our delegation that the temperature would have to cool down by ten degrees or so, or else it would be too hard on all of us. Sure enough, it cooled down by just that much when we arrived, and it never once rained right before or after the lectures as people were going back and forth. You can say the gods and dragons of the eightfold division have been most cooperative.

"You may consider this strange or incredible, but 'If you do not regard the strange as strange, the strange then is of itself defeated.' The world is vast. Just as everybody's visage is different, so is their wisdom and capacity for knowledge. I hope all of you will sit more in meditation. From meditation comes concentration and from concentration arises wisdom.

"In every situation, use your own wisdom to discriminate and do not follow anyone or anything blindly. Don't flow with the dust. Tonight my last words to you are: I vow that all of you – whoever hears my voice or sees my face, or indirectly hears my name – will become Buddhas soon. I will wait in the Saha world until all of you have accomplished Buddhahood, and then, if it is right for me, I'll also become a Buddha. If it isn't – well – that's okay too, I'm still happy."

Heng Sure • September 26, 1978
That's my skill, to cheat people

Favorite images.

Like the Buddha holding a flower up to the Assembly, wordlessly transmitting the Mind Dharma, the Abbot at his farewell banquet in Penang holds the microphone aloft, smiling a big grin. He brings it down and asks,

"Did you hear? Do you understand?"

Mahakashyapa smiled.

The Abbot's lecture:

"When I lived in Hong Kong my hair turned white, because I had too many false thoughts. I went to war inside my head all the time. People said, 'Oh, that Tu Lun! He's a *kuai wu* (monster).' Everyone was afraid of me. I used to scold everyone I met. I liked to hassle people most of all. I was an asura. My motto was 'The straight mind is the Bodhimanda.' But it didn't work out. No one drew near me. For a Dharma Master to scare everyone away is not the way to do it. You should not fight inside your mind.

"So when I got to America I put it all down. I mastered the *gung fu* of having no false thoughts. This is the best. And my hair turned black again, don't you know? I changed my ways. I never fight now, not with anyone. I've controlled my temper. Oh, there are some disciples who are still afraid of me, but most of them see through me – they know I'm a paper tiger. One puff of air and I'm blown over.

"I've cheated all these stupid Americans. They believe in me. They're as stupid as their teacher, and they imitate his stupid ways.

That's my skill, to cheat people. I lecture sutras even though I'm illiterate in English, but since they've never heard sutras lectured before, they don't know the difference. So I fool them like this. Now a bunch of them have tagged along with me to Asia and since they speak English they now trick all the Chinese people in turn." (laughter and cheers)

The Abbot: "As for speaking the Dharma, if you have real *gung fu* and truly cultivate, no matter what you say you can still influence people to bring forth the resolve for Bodhi. If you haven't any cultivation, then no matter how well you speak, no one benefits from it."

Heng Chau • September 26, 1978
This is just how the mad mind works

"You should all be here as if not here – don't think about leaving. When you go don't think about staying. Produce the mind that dwells nowhere." (The Abbot at a layperson's house.)

Kuo Ts'ai, sitting on the smelly stairs outside the Buddhist Lecture Hall in Hong Kong, looking forlorn or homesick: "Oh. it's just that I could still see staying on Lantau Island." Lantau Island is quiet, pastoral, with no hassles – the opposite of Hong Kong with its noise, crowds, and constant friction. It took me a long time to see the truth in the Abbot's statement that somewhere in cultivation the place is reached where all outside and inside conditions and states become level and equal. "Who would have guessed that the best area (*chi* point) is the square inch?" commented the Abbot in Los Angeles about the limits of *feng shui* in bringing happiness.

This state has to be experienced directly, because it doesn't make sense in the way we normally figure things. Some things are good, some are bad; the cities and mountains are as different as men and women – or so it seems.

No amount of words or debate can decide this issue. However you see it, that's how it is. But if you can understand how one day you can love someone and the next day hate the same person, or one minute feel ecstatic and the next depressed, then you've grasped the principle at work: "Everything is made from the mind alone."

To Kuo Ts'ai, Lantau Island is far preferable to Hong Kong as a place to cultivate and live. And yet sometimes when he is single-mindedly absorbed in his recitation of Guan Yin Bodhisattva no such thought of discrimination arises. When the recitation stops, Hong Kong and Lantau return with likes and dislikes. This is just how the mad mind works and from it the ten thousand things are born. "When the mad mind stops, just this stopping is Bodhi." It doesn't make sense right off. You've got to limber up and practice a bit. You've got to become a little weird and stupid, which is a fine way to be, because being "straight" is not much fun. The Bodhisattva is a weirdo who is happy, pure, and cool because,

"He understands that all dharmas are just like echoes. Regarding all of them, he is completely without attachment."

Ten Transferences Chapter
Avatamsaka Sutra

Heng Sure • September 27, 1978
Day 61 : Hong Kong / San Francisco

There's no place like Hong Kong for giving me the resolve to leave the red dust behind. Everything that's wrong with human beings takes the center stage in Hong Kong. All of our flaws appear in bold relief. Intense, ugly, unadorned. All levels of society share the same sickness, from the hideously stark poverty of Horse Mountain Village to the theatrical opulence of the Royal Hong Kong Jockey Club.

Any desire can be filled on the spot. Any small seed of evil can flourish in Hong Kong's fertile soil of human decay. Wealth, sex, fame, food, sleep, sugar, alcohol, meat, tobacco, drugs, lust, fighting, gambling, stealing, killing – all the bad things that people put in their mouths and do to each other – all are here on the streets, in the pent-houses, in the offices.

Kuo Ts'ai: "Kuo Kuei and I went to the shipping firm to pack off all our boxes of freight. There was a real stack of stuff. Before we left the Lecture Hall, the Abbot handed Kuo Kuei an unspecified sum of cash and off we went.

"We found the right place and then negotiated all the terms of the deal with weights, discounts, exchange taxes and all. Kuo Kuei pulled out the money the Abbot had given him and do you know what? It was the exact amount down to one Hong Kong dollar. It blew our minds!"

On our way back to America.

Late entries as journey ends: So careful and clean in the "deepest *yin* Hong Kong," ha! On the airplane I totally threw in the towel and got doused with sugar five times, sneaked glances at a sticky film, got hung up on my empty belly after a light lunch, read two magazines, and then overate like a madman on all the available food that the Abbot passed out like a blizzard. With a little concentration I could have turned it into a decent lunch. Nope. I wolfed down mooncakes, peanut butter and jelly sandwiches, spoiling tofu, *bau dz* (drew the line at the sweet ones) and then ate the airplane breakfast, too. Heavy belly! A false thought I'd eaten in my mind for about three days. What an empty farce!

Heng Chau • September 27, 1978
I know now what's true can seem so weird

Thoughts on *T'ai Chi.*

There are eighty-four thousand Dharma doors to the "dharma-less Dharma" of no attachments and no false thoughts. Whichever one unkinks it for you is number one and the best method. None are better or worse, good or bad.

T'ai Chi is a tool, a dharma, but is not ultimate. Among people there is no room for fault-finding, competition and slighting. All dharmas are level and equal and non-existent. Their nature is ultimately no nature.

Everything speaks the Dharma. True principle is within the self-nature, not outside. Tai Chi systems, for example, differ, but the principles are the same.

I've never been able to see this before. I always got defensive and absolute about my dharma and critical and fault-finding toward others. George Hu once said, "All the arts in their higher expressions are the same (non-dual)." It's people that make them different by their sincerity and diligent practice. It's like differences among religions or the vehicles in Buddhism. The source and end are one – everything between is temporary and a tool.

Leaving Hong Kong.

Merrily, merrily, merrily, merrily,
    Life is but a dream.

The eyes see form, but inside there is nothing,
The ears hear the dusty sounds,
    but the mind is not moved by them.

Since the transit room in Manila and leaving Hong Kong two months later, the truth of these lines has finally sunk in. Without attaching to emptiness, it is all like a dream. Without clinging to existence, form and sounds pass by like clouds, like time.

Before my eyes would get red from the dust and I would be turned by pretty women, how people saw me (us), the clock, and so forth. Ever since Malacca it's been slowly turning into a bright light and cool breeze. Two months near the Abbot and bowing in Asia has been a lot of suffering and a lot of learning – all toward the good for everyone.

Each one of us is changed – a little cleaner. The trip is just the continuing session that opened in America in 1968 with the Abbot's lecturing the Shurangama Sutra in San Francisco, and this Dharma Assembly in America is just a continuation of the Assembly that began when Shakyamuni Buddha opened enlightenment some 3000 years ago. How strange, and how wonderful!

Last-minute garland thoughts – flying back.

My taste for a lot of things has changed dramatically within the last two years – food, women, clothes, sleep, fame and name. It feels so good and healthy and natural to be this new way, but I know to the world it looks weird beyond imagination – and yet… watching a young stewardess stare at Kuo Jing, her world stopping, wondering and attracted, scared and reflective. She saw in Kuo Jing some secret deep place within herself – a spiritual mirror. It was great to see a real face peek through the make-up and airline school smile.

We are all doing an ultimately natural thing. On the flight back I smiled and cried a little in happiness to be on the right track again – the right way to live, close to nature. I also saw clearly how far away I had drifted and how unhappy and lonely I was at heart, rolling around in the red dust, trying to be #1. All the times I was successful and doing the "right things" left me with a longing for the peace of mind and integrity of what I am now – a monk.

So, I know now how lost one can get and how what's true can seem so weird and what's false can be worshipped and accepted so blindly. Especially during these last two months, my tastes have changed, and I'm not going back any more. I'll take the wind and light as my share. In taste there is no dispute. I've never felt cleaner or more honest about anything as I do about this. However strange it may seem, it's my original home. The immigration officer said a lot more than she realized when she said, "Oh yeah, and welcome home!"

Malacca somehow was a turning point. I've never been so close to death. For a day I felt doubt about what I am doing, but it passed with the poison. Since then, each day I feel stronger and more solid in the Way. There's just a growing bright light. I feel like a piece of pottery that all the bubbles have been beaten out of. Now the kiln can burn long and hot. I just get more durable and happy.

* * * * * * * * *
U.S.A.

Heng Sure • September 28, 1978
Overwhelming!

First impression of Americans – U.S. Customs people in the San Francisco Airport: sexual desire run wild! Clothes, ornaments, perfumes, body postures – all designed with the idea of attracting a mate. Overwhelming! Television and the cinema's influence! Cut off sexual desire and ninety percent of the Americans we meet will be turned. This is where we live.

Heng Chau • September 28, 1978
Clean food, clear mind

Gold Mountain – the nicest temple yet! Clean, simple, cold, and clear – everything about it says, "Shine within."

Readjustment – lots of fire from travelling and waves of fatigue. Food at Gold Mountain Monastery is fuel for cultivation. It tastes real good after months of gourmet and sweet treats. Clean food, clear mind. Another planet, an ageless space station on the mind ground.

A dream of the delegation in the U.S.: playful samadhi together, happy and recognizing each other beyond sex or age – deep old Dharma friends.

Heng Sure • September 29, 1978
Blessings have an end, just like money

The Malaysian miles. We bowed the equivalent of thirty miles while in Asia. Back home now and walking off those thirty miles of highway before we begin to bow again. Seaside, Sand City, Marina, and acres and miles of artichoke fields. Castroville, "artichoke capitol of the world," held its annual Artichoke Festival three weeks ago. They had a beauty queen contest, an artichoke gobbling contest (no doubt), and most likely a door prize of all the artichokes you can eat for life, pickled, french fried, baked, stuffed, and made into ice-cream.

Americans are rich in natural wealth, full of blessings from merit and virtue done in the past. Our fields of blessings were well planted and cared for. Now our fields of artichokes and orchards of avocados and all the abundant produce that grows along California's coastal highway testify to a history of good cultivation.

Nothing is fixed, however, especially with regard to cultivating wholesome deeds. Although we now enjoy the fruits of past efforts, Americans must recognize that our lives have become too comfortable, too pleasurable. Blessings have an end, just like money in a bank account. If one only withdraws the cash and makes no deposits, the wealth soon disappears.

> To endure suffering is to end suffering;
> To enjoy blessings exhausts blessings.

Where will we be in the future if we don't use effort in our own cultivation, working hard to benefit others? We have so much wealth that we have gone soft as a nation. At the same time, most of the world's citizens know hunger and malnutrition as a way of life.

Who cares? Aren't starving people getting the rewards they deserve just as we now are receiving our rightful benefits? Yes, cause and effect works just like that. "As you sow, so shall you reap." The point is not to be short-sighted. We can become the starving and needy ones very quickly. Why do people lack food? Because they were lazy and wasteful in the past. We are planting our fields now for future harvests – what kind of a crop will it be?

In Asia, arable land is scarce. Every inch is put to use all year. Fertilizer and water are precious – the growing cycle is not as distant from the eyes and minds of the citizens as in the West. The vegetables in the wok at lunch were grown in the field next door, for the most part. Yesterday's rice turned into feces is reclaimed for fertilizer today to grow tomorrow's rice. Nothing is wasted – nothing is hidden away.

It would be wise for us to recognize cause and effect and plan for a happy future for everyone.

Heng Chau • September 29, 1978
We'll make it past Marina today

Heng Shun drives us back to Monterey. Heng Sure walks off thirty miles (seventy-five percent of Asia bowing) through Fort Ord on Old Highway 1. I drive ahead, clock the distance, meditate.

How fine to be back in the wind and sun: Back to our simple meals, quiet days, and a different home every night. We'll make it past Marina today and Watsonville by the weekend. Bowing is our home, and dwelling nowhere is our work.

Heng Sure • September 30, 1978
Outside Moss Landing

Passed a giant power plant in morning fog. Bright-sailed schooners and ketches tied to piers. Fog clears, Officer Hugh Taylor and friend find us bivouacked beside a big rock on the edge of an artichoke field. Tofu and bean sprouts. "I enjoyed the magazine *Vajra Bodhi Sea* your Monastery sent. I'm going to write for a book catalog and read more Sutras," said Hugh.

Hiked 7.3 miles in tennis shoes with stiff soles. Arch supports bruised my instep but I was so wired and eager to begin bowing again I forced the walk and didn't notice the pain 'til I stopped.

Left Highway 1 where it turns into a freeway. Took the farming roads. Passed chicken houses, four mushrooms ranches, and a field of strawberry pickers. Waved to elder farmer on his tractor, he tips hat back, dark look melts to happy nod and two fingers to hat-brim salute. Monks counting paces on beads are an unusual sight.

Fog descends at dusk filling dark furrows closing in around the Plymouth. Cross the Santa Cruz County Line as the mist closes in. We can hear the local Watsonville High School marching band across the fields as we make camp.

> "At that time the Youth Good Wealth… contemplated the Way, specifically he contemplated the highs and lows of the Way, he contemplated the safety and perils of the Way, he contemplated the purities and defilements of the Way, he contemplated the crookedness and straightness of the Way."
>
> Entering the Dharma Realm
> Avatamsaka Sutra

Heng Chau • September 30, 1978
Everything comes from what you do

Noon – Moss Landing: Heng Sure walked off 7.3 miles. Impression: America/Asia. It depends on the point of view whether you think life is easier/better in Asia or America. On the surface, the contrast is glaring – lots of leisure time vs. working seven days a week to get by; overweight vs. hand to mouth; boredom is a result of surfeit; the young people in Asia start to work at a young age and never stop – young people in America can delay facing work well into their twenties and often altogether.

The pursuit of pleasure and desire-seeking is the pulse beat we felt in the airport when we landed, and it hasn't let up all the way to the highway we bow along. Scarcity and the bare essentials of food, clothing, and shelter is the pulse of Asia. Children go naked until the last socially permitted minute because clothes cost money. Sex in Asia breeds children. Sex in America breeds money. Involution of leisure, desire gone mad. Asia is full of suffering. America is over-flowing with blessings.

So what? Under the surface there's a principle at work that levels all differences. If what you do with your blessings is to selfishly seek small pleasures, then in the future you will undergo suffering. If you don't understand the causes of suffering (greed, anger, ignorance, stinginess, jealousy, etc.), then you'll never end suffering. The point is that suffering and blessings are just different sides of the same coin: everything that happens to you comes from what you do.

Suffering isn't fixed. One can change suffering into blessings. Blessings can quickly turn into suffering as well. It all depends on what you do. Everything changes, nothing stays the same.

Americans with a cushion of blessings could easily use them to cultivate the Way. With leisure time and the necessities provided for they could change their blessings into merit and virtue.

An old man in Singapore: "I'm retired. My children are all on their own. I don't have much money and I don't need much, so I'm free and happy. I'm using this time to learn about Buddhism and how to meditate. I don't want to waste this time playing checkers and waiting to die."

Hugh Taylor, a police officer in Monterey, uses his spare time to study Buddhadharma. He goes to weekend seminars and retreats. He reads sutras at home instead of watching television and drinking beer. He says,

"I'm still getting more and more excited by it. Christianity just didn't have anything for me."

> Buddhism and the art of becoming a person
>   are the same thing.
> Way-virtue is the art of being a human being.

Venerable Master Hsuan Hua

Buddhist Text Translation Society Publication

Buddhist Text Translation Society
International Translation Institute

http://www.bttsonline.org

1777 Murchison Drive,
Burlingame, California 94010-4504 USA
Phone: (650) 692-5912 Fax: (650) 692-5056

When Buddhism first came to China from India, one of the most important tasks required for its establishment was the translation of the Buddhist scriptures from Sanskrit into Chinese. This work involved a great many people, such as the renowned monk National Master Kumarajiva (fifth century), who led an assembly of over 800 people to work on the translation of the Tripitaka (Buddhist canon) for over a decade. Because of the work of individuals such as these, nearly the entire Buddhist Tripitaka of over a thousand texts exists to the present day in Chinese.

Now the banner of the Buddha's teachings is being firmly planted in Western soil, and the same translation work is being done from Chinese into English. Since 1970, the Buddhist Text Translation Society (BTTS) has been making a paramount contribution toward this goal. Aware that the Buddhist Tripitaka is a work of such magnitude that its translation could never be entrusted to a single person, the BTTS, emulating the translation assemblies of ancient times, does not publish a work until it has passed through four committees for primary translation, revision, editing, and certification. The leaders of these committees are Bhikshus (monks) and Bhikshunis (nuns) who have devoted their lives to the study and practice of the Buddha's teachings. For this reason, all of the works of the BTTS put an emphasis on what the principles of the Buddha's teachings mean in terms of actual practice and not simply hypothetical conjecture.

The translations of canonical works by the Buddhist Text Translation Society are accompanied by extensive commentaries by the Venerable Tripitaka Master Hsuan Hua.

BTTS Publications

Buddhist Sutras. Amitabha Sutra, Dharma Flower (Lotus) Sutra, Flower Adornment (Avatamsaka) Sutra, Heart Sutra & Verses without a Stand, Shurangama Sutra, Sixth Patriarch Sutra, Sutra in Forty-two Sections, Sutra of the Past Vows of Earth Store Bodhisattva, Vajra Prajna Paramita (Diamond) Sutra.

Commentarial Literature. Buddha Root Farm, City of 10 000 Buddhas Recitation Handbook, Filiality: The Human Source, Herein Lies the Treasure-trove, Listen to Yourself Think Everything Over, Shastra on the Door to Understanding the Hundred Dharmas, Song of Enlightenment, The Ten Dharma Realms Are Not Beyond a Single Thought, Venerable Master Hua's Talks on Dharma, Venerable Master Hua's Talks on Dharma during the 1993 Trip to Taiwan, Water Mirror Reflecting Heaven.

Biographical. In Memory of the Venerable Master Hsuan Hua, Pictorial Biography of the Venerable Master Hsü Yün, Records of High Sanghans, Records of the Life of the Venerable Master Hsüan Hua, Three Steps One Bow, World Peace Gathering, News from True Cultivators, Open Your Eyes Take a Look at the World, With One Heart Bowing to the City of 10 000 Buddhas.

Children's Books. Cherishing Life, Human Roots: Buddhist Stories for Young Readers, Spider Web, Giant Turtle, Patriarch Bodhidharma.

Musics, Novels and Brochures. Songs for Awakening, Awakening, The Three Cart Patriarch, City of 10 000 Buddhas Color Brochure, Celebrisi's Journey, Lots of Time Left.

The Buddhist Monthly–Vajra Bodhi Sea is a monthly journal of orthodox Buddhism which has been published by the Dharma Realm Buddhist Association, formerly known as the Sino-American Buddhist Association, since 1970. Each issue contains the most recent translations of the Buddhist canon by the Buddhist Text Translation Society. Also included in each issue are a biography of a great Patriarch of Buddhism from the ancient past, sketches of the lives of contemporary monastics and lay-followers around the world, articles on practice, and other material. The journal is bilingual, Chinese and English.

Please visit our web-site at **www.bttsonline.org** for the latest publications and for ordering information.

Dharma Realm Buddhist Association Branches

The City of Ten Thousand Buddhas
4951 Bodhi Way, Ukiah, CA 95482 USA
Tel: (707) 462-0939   Fax: (707) 462-0949
Website: **http://www.drba.org** Email: **cttb@drba.org**

Buddhist Text Translation Society Online Catalog
Website: **http://www.bttsonline.org**

Institute for World Religions (Berkeley Buddhist Monastery)
2304 McKinley Avenue, Berkeley, CA 94703 USA
Tel: (510) 848-3440 Fax: (510) 548-4551 Email: paramita@drba.org

Dharma Realm Buddhist Books Distribution Society
11th Floor, 85 Chung-hsiao E. Road, Sec. 6, Taipei, Taiwan R.O.C.
Tel: (02) 2786-3022 Fax: (02) 2786-2674 Email: drbbds@ms1.seeder.net

The City of the Dharma Realm
1029 West Capitol Avenue, West Sacramento, CA 95691 USA
Tel: (916) 374-8268 Fax: (916) 374-8234 Email: cdrclasses@yahoo.com

Gold Mountain Monastery
800 Sacramento Street, San Francisco, CA 94108 USA
Tel: (415) 421-6117 Fax: (415) 788-6001

Gold Wheel Monastery
235 North Avenue 58, Los Angeles, CA 90042 USA
Tel: (323) 258-6668 Fax: (323) 258-3619

Gold Buddha Monastery
248 East 11th Avenue, Vancouver, B.C. V5T 2C3 Canada
Tel: (604) 709-0248 Fax: (604) 684-3754 Email: drab@gbm-online.com
Website: http://www.drba/gbm-online.com

Gold Summit Monastery
233 1st Avenue, West Seattle, WA 98119 USA
Tel: (206) 284-6690 Fax: (206) 284-6918
Website: http://www.goldsummitmonastery.org

Gold Sage Monastery
11455 Clayton Road, San Jose, CA 95127-5099 USA
Tel: (408) 923-7243 Fax: (408) 923-1064

The International Translation Institute
1777 Murchison Drive, Burlingame, CA 94010-4504 USA
Tel: (650) 692-5912 Fax: (650) 692-5056

Long Beach Monastery
3361 East Ocean Boulevard, Long Beach, CA 90803 USA
Tel: (562) 438-8902

Blessings, Prosperity, & Longevity Monastery
4140 Long Beach Boulevard, Long Beach, CA 90807 USA
Tel: (562) 595-4966

Avatamsaka Vihara
9601 Seven Locks Road, Bethesda, MD 20817-9997, USA
Tel/Fax: (301) 469-8300 Email: hwa_yean88@msn.com

Avatamsaka Monastery
1009 4th Avenue, S.W. Calgary, AB T2P OK8 Canada
Tel: (403) 234-0644 Fax: (403) 263-0537
Website: http://www.avatamsaka.ca

Dharma Realm Guanyin Sagely Monastery
161, Jalan Ampang, 50450 Kuala Lumpur, West Malaysia
Tel: (03) 2164-8055 Fax: (03) 2163-7118

Prajna Guanyin Sagely Monastery (formerly Tze Yun Tung)
Batu 5½, Jalan Sungai Besi, Salak Selatan, 57100 Kuala Lumpur, Malaysia
Tel: (03) 7982-6560 Fax: (03) 7980-1272

Lotus Vihara
136, Jalan Sekolah, 45600 Batang Berjuntai, Selangor Darul Ehsan, Malaysia
Tel: (03) 3271-9439

Source of Dharma Realm – Lot S130, 2nd Floor, Green Zone, Sungai Wang
Plaza, Jalan Bukit Bintang, 55100 Kuala Lumpur, Malaysia
Tel: (03) 2164-8055

Buddhist Lecture Hall – 31 Wong Nei Chong Road, Top Floor, Happy
Valley, Hong Kong, China
Tel: (02) 2572-7644 Fax: (2) 2572-2850

Dharma Realm Sagely Monastery – 20, Tong-hsi Shan-chuang, Hsing-lung
Village, Liu-kuei Kaohsiung County, Taiwan, R.O.C.
Tel: (07) 689-3717 Fax: (07) 689-3870

Amitabha Monastery – 7, Su-chien-hui, Chih-nan Village, Shou-feng,
Hualien County, Taiwan, R.O.C.
Tel: (07) 865-1956 Fax: (07) 865-3426

Gold Coast Dharma Realm
106 Bonogin Road, Mudgeeraba, Queensland 4213 Australia
Tel/fax: (07) 61-755-228-788 (07) 61-755-227-822

The Dharma Realm Buddhist Association

Mission

The Dharma Realm Buddhist Association (formerly the Sino-American Buddhist Association) was founded by the Venerable Master Hsuan Hua in the United States of America in 1959. Taking the Dharma Realm as its scope, the Association aims to disseminate the genuine teachings of the Buddha throughout the world. The Association is dedicated to translating the Buddhist canon, propagating the Orthodox Dharma, promoting ethical education, and bringing benefit and happiness to all beings. Its hope is that individuals, families, the society, the nation, and the entire world will, under the transforming influence of the Buddhadharma, gradually reach the state of ultimate truth and goodness.

The Founder

The Venerable Master, whose names were An Tse and To Lun, received the Dharma name Hsuan Hua and the transmission of Dharma from Venerable Master Hsu Yun in the lineage of the Wei Yang Sect. He was born in Manchuria, China, at the beginning of the century. At nineteen, he entered the monastic order and dwelt in a hut by his mother's grave to practice filial piety. He meditated, studied the teachings, ate only one meal a day, and slept sitting up. In 1948 he went to Hong Kong, where he established the Buddhist Lecture Hall and other Way-places. In 1962 he brought the Proper Dharma to the West, lecturing on several dozen Mahayana Sutras in the United States. Over the years, the Master established more than twenty monasteries of Proper Dharma under the auspices of the Dharma Realm Buddhist Association and the City of Ten Thousand Buddhas. He also founded centers for the translation of the Buddhist canon and for education to spread the influence of the Dharma in the East and West. The Master manifested the stillness in the United States in 1995. Through his lifelong, selfless dedication to teaching living beings with wisdom and compassion, he influenced countless people to change their faults and to walk upon the pure, bright path to enlightenment.

Dharma Propagation, Buddhist Text Translation, and Education

The Venerable Master Hua's three great vows after leaving the home-life were (1) to propagate the Dharma, (2) to translate the Buddhist Canon, and (3) to promote education. In order to make these vows a reality, the Venerable Master based himself on the Three Principles and the Six Guidelines. Courageously facing every hardship, he founded monasteries, schools, and centers in the West, drawing in living beings and teaching them on a vast scale. Over the years, he founded the following institutions:

The City of Ten Thousand Buddhas and Its Branches

In propagating the Proper Dharma, the Venerable Master not only trained people but also founded Way-places where the Dharma wheel could turn and living beings could be saved. He wanted to provide cultivators with pure places to practice in accord with the Buddha's regulations. Over the years, he founded many Way-places of Proper Dharma. In the United States and Canada, these include the City of Ten Thousand Buddhas; Gold Mountain Monastery; Gold Sage Monastery; Gold Wheel Monastery; Gold Summit Monastery; Gold Buddha Monastery; Avatamsaka Monastery; Long Beach Monastery; the City of the Dharma Realm; Berkeley Buddhist Monastery; Avatamsaka Hermitage; and Blessings, Prosperity, and Longevity Monastery. In Taiwan, there are the Dharma Realm Buddhist Books Distribution Association, Dharma Realm Monastery, and Amitabha Monastery. In Malaysia, there are the Prajna Guanyin Sagely Monastery (formerly Tze Yun Tung Temple), Deng Bi An Monastery, and Lotus Vihara. In Hong Kong, there are the Buddhist Lecture Hall and Cixing Monastery.

Purchased in 1974, the City of Ten Thousand Buddhas is the hub of the Dharma Realm Buddhist Association. The City is located in Talmage, Mendocino County, California, 110 miles north of San Francisco. Eighty of the 488 acres of land are in active use. The remaining acreage consists of meadows, orchards, and woods. With over seventy large buildings containing over 2,000 rooms, blessed with serenity and fresh, clean air, it is the first large Buddhist monastic community in the United States. It is also an international center for the Proper Dharma.

Although the Venerable Master Hua was the Ninth Patriarch in the Wei Yang Sect of the Chan School, the monasteries he founded emphasize all of the five main practices of Mahayana Buddhism (Chan meditation, Pure Land, esoteric, Vinaya (moral discipline), and doctrinal studies). This accords with the Buddha's words: "The Dharma is level and equal, with no high or low." At the City of Ten Thousand Buddhas, the rules of purity are rigorously observed. Residents of the City strive to regulate their own conduct and to cultivate with vigor. Taking refuge in the Proper Dharma, they lead pure and selfless lives, and attain peace in body and mind. The Sutras are expounded and the Dharma wheel is turned daily. Residents dedicate themselves wholeheartedly to making Buddhism flourish. Monks and nuns in all the monasteries take one meal a day, always wear their precept sash, and follow the Three Principles:

> *Freezing, we do not scheme.*
> *Starving, we do not beg.*
> *Dying of poverty, we ask for nothing.*
> *According with conditions, we do not change.*
> *Not changing, we accord with conditions.*
> *We adhere firmly to our three great principles.*
> *We renounce our lives to do the Buddha's work.*
> *We take the responsibility to mold our own destinies.*
> *We rectify our lives to fulfill the Sanghan's role.*
> *Encountering specific matters,*
> *   we understand the principles.*
> *Understanding the principles,*
> *   we apply them in specific matters.*
> *We carry on the single pulse of*
> *   the Patriarchs' mind-transmission.*

The monasteries also follow the Six Guidelines: not contending, not being greedy, not seeking, not being selfish, not pursuing personal advantage, and not lying.

International Translation Institute

The Venerable Master vowed to translate the Buddhist Canon (Tripitaka) into Western languages so that it would be widely accessible throughout the world. In 1973, he founded the International Translation Institute on Washington Street in San Francisco for the purpose of translating Buddhist scriptures into English and other languages. In 1977, the Institute was merged into Dharma Realm Buddhist University as the Institute for the Translation of Buddhist Texts. In 1991, the Venerable Master purchased a large building in Burlingame (south of San Francisco) and established the International Translation Institute there for the purpose of translating and publishing Buddhist texts. To date, in addition to publishing over one hundred volumes of Buddhist texts in Chinese, the Association has published more than one hundred volumes of English, French, Spanish, Vietnamese, and Japanese translations of Buddhist texts, as well as bilingual (Chinese and English) editions. Audio and video tapes also continue to be produced. The monthly journal Vajra Bodhi Sea, which has been in circulation for nearly thirty years, has been published in bilingual (Chinese and English) format in recent years.

In the past, the difficult and vast mission of translating the Buddhist canon in China was sponsored and supported by the emperors and kings themselves. In our time, the Venerable Master encouraged his disciples to cooperatively shoulder this heavy responsibility, producing books and audio tapes and using the medium of language to turn the wheel of Proper Dharma and do the great work of the Buddha. All those who aspire to devote themselves to this work of sages should uphold the Eight Guidelines of the International Translation Institute:

1. One must free oneself from the motives of personal fame and profit.

2. One must cultivate a respectful and sincere attitude free from arrogance and conceit.

3. One must refrain from aggrandizing one's work and denigrating that of others.

4. One must not establish oneself as the standard of correctness and suppress the work of others with one's fault-finding.

5. One must take the Buddha-mind as one's own mind.

6. One must use the wisdom of Dharma-Selecting Vision to determine true principles.

7. One must request Virtuous Elders of the ten directions to certify one's translations.

8. One must endeavor to propagate the teachings by printing Sutras, Shastra texts, and Vinaya texts when the translations are certified as being correct.

These are the Venerable Master's vows, and participants in the work of translation should strive to realize them.

Instilling Goodness Elementary School, Developing Virtue Secondary School, Dharma Realm Buddhist University

"Education is the best national defense." The Venerable Master Hua saw clearly that in order to save the world, it is essential to promote good education. If we want to save the world, we have to bring about a complete change in people's minds and guide them to cast out unwholesomeness and to pursue goodness. To this end the Master founded Instilling Goodness Elementary School in 1974, and Developing Virtue Secondary School and Dharma Realm Buddhist University in 1976.

In an education embodying the spirit of Buddhism, the elementary school teaches students to be filial to parents, the secondary school teaches students to be good citizens, and the university teaches such virtues as humaneness and righteousness. Instilling Goodness Elementary School and Developing Virtue Secondary School combine the best of contemporary and traditional methods and of Western and Eastern cultures. They emphasize moral virtue and spiritual development, and aim to guide students to become good and capable citizens who will benefit humankind. The schools offer a bilingual (Chinese/English) program where boys and girls study separately. In addition to standard academic courses, the curriculum includes ethics, meditation, Buddhist studies, and so on, giving students a foundation in virtue and guiding them to understand themselves and explore the truths of the universe. Branches of the schools (Sunday schools) have been established at branch monasteries with the aim of propagating filial piety and ethical education.

Dharma Realm Buddhist University, whose curriculum focuses on the Proper Dharma, does not merely transmit academic knowledge. It emphasizes a foundation in virtue, which expands into the study of how to help all living beings discover their inherent nature. Thus, Dharma Realm Buddhist University advocates a spirit of shared inquiry and free exchange of ideas, encouraging students to study various canonical texts and use different experiences and learning styles to tap their inherent wisdom and fathom the meanings of those texts. Students are encouraged to practice the principles they have understood and apply the Buddhadharma in their lives, thereby nurturing their wisdom and virtue. The University aims to produce outstanding individuals of high moral character who will be able to bring benefit to all sentient beings.

Sangha and Laity Training Programs

In the Dharma-ending Age, in both Eastern and Western societies there are very few monasteries that actually practice the Buddha's regulations and strictly uphold the precepts. Teachers with genuine wisdom and understanding, capable of guiding those who aspire to pursue careers in Buddhism, are very rare. The Venerable Master founded the Sangha and Laity Training Programs in 1982 with the goals of raising the caliber of the Sangha, perpetuating the Proper Dharma, providing professional training for Buddhists around the world on both practical and theoretical levels, and transmitting the wisdom of the Buddha.

The Sangha Training Program gives monastics a solid foundation in Buddhist studies and practice, training them in the practical affairs of Buddhism and Sangha management. After graduation, students will be able to assume various responsibilities related to Buddhism in monasteries, institutions, and other settings. The program emphasizes a thorough knowledge of Buddhism, understanding of the scriptures, earnest cultivation, strict observance of precepts, and the development of a virtuous character, so that students will be able to propagate the Proper Dharma and perpetuate the Buddha's wisdom. The Laity Training Program offers courses to help laypeople develop correct views, study and practice the teachings, and understand monastic regulations and ceremonies, so that they will be able to contribute their abilities in Buddhist organizations.

Let Us Go Forward Together

In this Dharma-ending Age when the world is becoming increasingly dangerous and evil, the Dharma Realm Buddhist Association, in consonance with its guiding principles, opens the doors of its monasteries and centers to those of all religions and nationalities. Anyone who is devoted to humaneness, righteousness, virtue, and the pursuit of truth, and who wishes to understand him or herself and help humankind, is welcome to come study and practice with us. May we together bring benefit and happiness to all living beings.

Verse of Transference

May the merit and virtue accrued from this work,
Adorn the Buddhas' Pure Lands,
Repaying four kinds of kindness above,
And aiding those suffering in the paths below.

May those who see and hear of this,
All bring forth the resolve for Bodhi,
And when this retribution body is over,
Be born together in the Land of Ultimate Bliss.

Dharma Protector Wei Tuo Bodhisattva